The Essential Attributes of God

The Essential Attributes of God

W M Banks

T Bentley

A W Foster

E Griffiths

I Jackson

CHALLENGER *Publishing*®

"Let us rise up and build". Neh. 2.18

Published by Challenger Publishing

Edited by Drew Marshall and David E West
Cover Design: *'En ar-che'* - B.W. Chalmers

Printed in Great Britain by Bell & Bain Ltd., Glasgow

ISBN: 0-9541240-0-6

Challenger Publishing
3 Netherton Place
Whitburn W. Lothian
Scotland EH47 8JG

CONTENTS

FOREWORD

In the so-called High Priestly prayer of the Lord Jesus, addressed to His Father, He says, "And this is life eternal, that they might **know** Thee the only true God, and Jesus Christ, whom Thou hast sent" (Jn. 17.3).

There is no greater knowledge than the knowledge of God and of His Son, Jesus Christ, concerning whom it is written, "No man hath seen God at any time; the only begotten Son, which is in the bosom of the Father, He hath declared Him (i.e. told Him out)" (Jn. 1.18).

Although "His eternal power and Godhead" (Rom. 1.20) have been revealed in creation, nevertheless, it is through His Word, by the power of the Holy Spirit, that we are enabled to come to a **knowledge of God**.

Have we, as believers, lost a sense of the glory and the greatness and the majesty of God? A careful consideration of The Essential Attributes of God, His Omniscience, His Omnipresence, His Omnipotence, His Immutability and His Eternity, as presented in this volume, will elevate our thoughts of God and cause our hearts to bow in worship before Him.

I am very happy to commend to you the reading of this book, dealing with subjects that are often overlooked and written by my esteemed brethren, William Banks, Thomas Bentley, Sandy Foster, Edward Griffiths and Ian Jackson, with all of whom I have had the privilege of sharing in the ministry of the word.

David E West

Leicester

July, 2001.

THE OMNISCIENCE OF GOD

By William M Banks

INTRODUCTION

The subject of the attributes of God has been addressed in many scholarly works in the past. However, for theological depth on a subject of this nature it seems necessary to go back several centuries! Modern writers tend to skip this important subject perhaps because of its complexity but maybe too because fewer readers take a real interest in it.

The early works are very erudite though the language tends to be a little dated. They are however, well worth the effort in studying them. The present contribution has leaned heavily on one of those important works (1). Stephen Charnock of the seventeenth century was evidently a man of outstanding spiritual calibre but also of high intellectual capacity. He had a deep understanding of biblical doctrinal issues and writes with an evident reverence. The following presentation has therefore unashamedly leaned heavily on this work.

DEFINITION

It is always necessary to define our terms and particularly so when dealing with a subject which is not commonly addressed. What is meant by an 'attribute' and what is meant by 'omniscience'?

An 'attribute' not surprisingly is something attributed to a person or thing. It essentially belongs to that person or the thing being considered. 'The attributes of God are those qualities or perfections of His nature which are its necessary characteristic and expression' (2). All Divine attributes are present in equal perfection and in a sense are not something really distinct from God Himself. However, in order to grasp their significance they are usually divided as far as human language is concerned so that we can understand a little their significance. One of these attributes is omniscience (see (2)).

In fine 'omniscience' is 'knowledge of all things' particularly in a universal context. There is nothing outside of God's knowledge. "His understanding is infinite" (Ps. 147.5). He knows; first and last, Alpha and Omega! He knows; not from experience but as an essential absolute attribute.

It is thus considered permissible to use the word 'knowledge' and its derivatives and synonyms as essentially interchangeable with 'omniscience'. Subsequent parts of this chapter will therefore take this liberty.

The subject is one of the most solemn and searching. Nothing is outwith God's cognisance, from the function of the atom to the workings of the universe, from the inward thought to the external action, from the motive to the movement, from the past to the future. "O the depth of the riches both of the wisdom and knowledge of God!" (Rom. 11.33).

THE NATURE AND EXTENT OF GOD'S KNOWLEDGE

It is essential initially to appreciate the nature of God's omniscience. **Remembrance** relates to things past. **Foreknowledge** relates to things future. **Knowledge** relates to things present. This present knowledge is related to wisdom and prudence. 'Wisdom is the flower of knowledge, and knowledge is the root of wisdom' (1).

REMEMBRANCE

The idea of remembrance is seen in the case of Noah. "And God remembered Noah" (Gen. 8.1). Not that He had forgotten His righteous servant during the days of the flood! The verb indicates that God knew the full details of the circumstances through which Noah was passing and lavished special attention and personal care upon him. The same idea is seen in relation to Samson (Judg. 16.28), Hannah (1 Sam. 1.11), Abraham (Gen. 19.29) and the repentant thief on the cross (Lk. 23.42). The same remembrance is available to His afflicted servants today!

"You only have I known of all the families of the earth …" God says to Israel through Amos (3.2). Not that His knowledge was limited! But His special love and care had been showered abundantly upon them and God expected a response in return. Privilege always brings responsibility. So today "the Lord knoweth them that are His" (2 Tim. 2.19). There is a corresponding responsibility … "Let every one that nameth the name of Christ depart from iniquity" (2 Tim. 2.19). It is good when apprehension leads to approbation.

On the contrary when God fails to approve He is said not to know; "I know you not" (Mt. 25.12) or "I never knew you" (Mt. 7.23). 'It is not an ignorance of understanding, but an ignorance of will' (1). The very fact that He gives the reason for rejecting them, namely having an awareness of their works ("… depart from Me, ye that work iniquity" (Mt. 7.23), indicates that an act of the Divine will is in question.

God's remembrance of all things past is absolute. He is the God of the "seven eyes" (Zech. 3.9) with perfection of vision and understanding.

Foreknowledge

God not only remembers all things past, He knows all things to come. (It is in this sense that foreknowledge is used here. The particular NT doctrine will be addressed later). Time is no barrier to God. For Him there is only one eternal present. He is the "I AM", before time, above time and beyond time. There is a sense therefore in which nothing is future for Him. In another sense, nothing can be future without Him.

He could not be responsible for the government of the universe without a knowledge of the future. Did He not know what was going to happen in Joseph's case? "Ye thought evil against me; but God meant it unto good, to bring to pass …" (Gen. 50.20), was Joseph's word to his brethren. Everything was under Divine control. And what shall we say of Moses, Samson, Ezekiel and many others? Did God not regulate the circumstances of their early lives to ensure His purposes were implemented for them and for the nation?

In addition the prediction of the future evidences His intimate knowledge of it. What is impenetrable to us is open and bare to Him whose eyes are "as a flame of fire" (Rev. 1.14). Is it not with irony that the supposed gods of the heathen are thus addressed, "Let them ... show us what shall happen: let them ... declare us things for to come ... that we may know that ye are gods" (Is. 41.22,23)? God knows and declares things to come! The idols know not; they are no gods! God could foretell the famine in Egypt, the captivity in Babylon, the rejection of the Jews, the calling of the Gentiles. But more, He could **name** individuals who would implement His decrees centuries before they came to pass e.g. 1Kings 13.2; Isaiah 44.28. Isn't it interesting that in the former case the instrument for the destruction of Jeroboam's altar should be none other than Amon's son Josiah (2 Kings 21.26)? For centuries not one of the kings of Judah called his son by the name Josiah. And yet a king who would have gladly propagated idolatry (and was free to choose his son's name) used the very name predicted by God in advance as the name which would be given to the king who would smash the idolatrous altar!

The **place** of Christ's birth, the **manner** of it, and its **timing** were also all specifically identified centuries in advance (Mic. 5.2, Is.7.14 and Dan. 9.25-27) not to mention the details of His life and death.

Knowledge

The Hebrew writer asserts unequivocally that "all things are naked and opened unto the eyes of Him with whom we have to do" (Heb. 4.13). There is nothing hidden from Him! Every **creature** from the least to the greatest, from the highest to the lowest is known to Him. "I know all the fowls (birds) of the mountains: and the wild beasts of the field are mine" (Ps.50.11). He provides food for the raven (Job 38.41) and for "his young ones". He numbers the clouds in His wisdom (Job 38.37), calls the stars by their names i.e. He knows every intimate detail about them; their orbit, temperature, composition etc. What scientists are only beginning to discover of the wonders of the universe are intimately known to Him!

In addition God knows the **activities** of His creatures. "Doth not He see my ways, and count all my steps?" (Job 31.4). He weighs them and assesses them by Divine standards. The words spoken by the King of Syria in his "bedchamber" were known by God and revealed to His prophet Elisha (2 Kings 6.12). However, He not only knows what men do but what they would have done had circumstances in their lives been different. For example Abimelech would have sinned had not God restrained him "I … withheld thee from sinning against Me: therefore suffered I thee not to touch her" (Gen. 20.6).

He knows how men and women who have never heard the gospel would react had the opportunity been granted to them. "Woe unto thee, Chorazin! woe unto thee, Bethsaida! for if the mighty works, which were done in you, had been done in Tyre and Sidon, they would have repented long ago in sackcloth and ashes" (Mt. 11.21). Such knowledge is too wonderful for us!

Also God knows the **thoughts** of His creatures. There is nothing impenetrable to Him. The inward motion, motives and debates are all known to Him. He assesses their significance. "The righteous God trieth the hearts and reins (inner man)" (Ps. 7.9). He is "a discerner of the thoughts and intents of the heart" (Heb. 4.12). Man is unable to hide behind pretence or excuse. God's eye sees everything. "Hell and destruction are before the Lord: how much more then the hearts of the children of men?" (Prov. 15.11). The God who knows the whole state of the dead is aware of the thoughts of the living! 'Not a secret in any soul in hell is hid from Him' (1). But further, He not only knows the thoughts, He knows the spring from which the thoughts come. "Thou understandest my thought afar off" (Ps. 139.2). The whole thought process from inception to implementation ('where the bird will light when it is in flight'(1)) is known to Him. The good motions of the mind; the evil motions of the mind are all discernable to Him. Peter could say "Lord, thou knowest all things; thou knowest that I love

Devil

whats outside a soul?

Thee" (Jn. 21.17). On the other hand God knows that relative to man in Noah's day "every imagination of the thoughts of his heart was only evil continually" (Gen. 6.5). Of course, without this knowledge God would not be a righteous judge. "I the Lord search the heart, I try the reins, even to give every man according to his ways, and according to the fruit of his doings" (Jer. 17.10).

THE KNOWLEDGE OF GOD IN SALVATION

In the context of salvation (used in its broadest sense) the omniscience of God is considered as from eternity. In a sense therefore all the details can be considered as future from a human perspective. It can not be appreciated otherwise. The fact that the word '**foreknowledge**' is used in this regard should thus not be surprising.

The idea in the word is however, much more than merely that of knowing in advance. The latter fact of course is true (as has been shown earlier) but to limit the word to that is far too restrictive. The true meaning as always is obtained by tracing its occurrence in its context in the New Testament.

The word in both its verb and noun form is found seven times in the New Testament. Two of these (Acts 26.5 and 2 Peter 3.17) are used of human knowledge based on prior experience and can be dismissed from further consideration here. The other five permit the meaning to be understood. The references in the verb form are to be found in Romans 8.29, Romans 11.2 and 1 Peter 1.20. The references in the noun form are to be found in Acts 2.23 and 1 Peter 1.2. A consideration of each reveals some interesting details.

Perhaps the most important reference for a true understanding of the meaning of the word is to be found in the context of 1 Peter 1.20. Here our Lord is referred to as the "Lamb … who verily was foreordained (foreknown) before the foundation of the world". It would clearly be unnecessary for the apostle to indicate that the Father knew the Lamb before the foundation of the world in the sense of mere prescience. In addition it would be inappropriate for Peter merely to inform his readers of this fact. That would not help them in the development of their thinking in the context of the argument the apostle is addressing. He is appealing for a lifestyle consistent with the gospel they have believed and the redemption they have experienced. The fact that the Lamb was known by the Father "before the foundation of the world" would not be a sufficient basis of appeal. This would be taken for granted by the readers!

However, to appreciate that the Godhead had planned the full concept of redemption in the 'counsels of eternity' and implemented it for their good in time by a definite fiat of the Divine will is different. This is surely what the apostle is affirming. The "foreknowing" was in effect the statement of a Divine purpose to implement the plan of redemption for the benefit of mankind in the death of the "Lamb". He foreknew because He had foreordained! 'God's foreknowledge is given here as the cause for His Son's sacrifice - because He planned and decreed it' (3).

It is perfectly in keeping with both the context of the passages and the meaning of the word to use the same idea in the other two verbal form references in Romans 8.29 and 11.2. In Romans 8.29 the apostle asserts "whom He did foreknow, He also did predestinate to be conformed to the image of His Son". The knowledge, or more accurately foreknowledge, is not of facts but persons! As the late Mr A E Leckie said, 'It is not that He knew facts about me but He knew me'. Thus again 'God foreknows because He has foreordained all things'.

The apostle is developing the eternal purpose of God in relation to the wellbeing of His own in Romans 8.29-30. It has an 'eternal perspective' leading to glorification. It is a fivefold chain of Divine purpose which cannot be broken - the "all things" working together for good to them that love God (v.28). And it all begins with foreknowledge! It leads through predestinating, calling, justifying to the glorifying. Note the recurrence of "whom" - once in verse 29 and three times in verse 30. Also the repetition of "them He also" - three times in verse 30. The apostle is carefully and clearly and concisely emphasising that persons are in view "whom ... whom ... whom ... whom"; "them ... them ...

them" - and that from eternity! Divine purpose from eternity was the blessing of persons in time and that for eternity! That believers should "... be conformed to the image of His Son, that He might be the firstborn among many brethren", is not based on anything they would do but solely on His foreknowledge.

However, His foreknowledge is not only individual in Romans 8 but national in Romans 11. The final reference to the verb form is in Romans 11.2 "God hath not cast away His people which He foreknew". No - the counsels of Deity will be implemented in relation to the nation as well. There was a remnant in Elijah's day - "Seven thousand men who have not bowed the knee to the image of Baal" (v.4). There was a remnant when Paul was writing - "Even so ... at this present time also there is a remnant according to the election of grace" (v.5). There will be a fullness of Divine blessing in the future! "All Israel shall be saved ... for the gifts and calling of God are without repentance" (vv.26,29). There is still a great future for the nation - undeserving though it is. God's counsels will be implemented in full!

The references in the noun form confirm the same truth detailed above. The first is found in Acts 2.23. The apostle Peter says of the Lord Jesus "Him being delivered by the determinate counsel and foreknowledge of God, ye have taken, and by wicked hands have crucified and slain". Herein lies a deep mystery! "Delivered by the ... foreknowledge of God"; "taken ... by wicked hands". There is clearly much more here than God merely knowing in advance that wicked hands would take His Son. His foreknowledge and determinate counsel are intimately linked. The deliberations of the Divine 'counsel' meant that the Son of God would die on Calvary's cross. It was not only foreknown, it was foreordained! How else could men "take" Him? They were utterly incapable of determining the time of His death (see e.g. Luke 4.29-30). It was in His own hand. They are nevertheless responsible for His death and will be accountable to God in the end. The prediction of His death 'was not the cause of their sin' but their sin was nevertheless foreseen.

The final reference in 1 Peter 1.2 is consistent with what has gone before. The "strangers scattered" were "elect according to the foreknowledge of God the Father". Their "sanctification of the Spirit, unto obedience" in time was due to the electing purpose of God in eternity. Salvation is all of God! It "belongeth unto Jehovah" (Ps. 3.8 RV) and apart from His initiative there would be no people for God. Thus 'believing is not the cause of their election. Election is the cause of their believing'. The late Mr J Hunter had an interesting definition - 'Election secures for God a people where otherwise there would be none'.

THE PRACTICAL IMPLICATION OF OMNISCIENCE - GODWARD

So far the subject has been looked at objectively. The truth has been defined and analysed. Its nature and extent and implications in the realm of salvation have been addressed. It would be inappropriate to exclude the implications subjectively. What use can the subject be put to practically? What instruction can we derive from such an important truth?

The implications are clearly diverse and searching. A number will be looked at in detail. If God is omniscient then He is **Supreme** in the realm of creation and redemption. He is **Sovereign** of the universe. He is **worthy of worship**.

God is Supreme

'He knows all things independently' (1). "Who ... being His counsellor hath taught Him?" (Is. 40.13). God is the source, the fountain of all knowledge. Every creature is thus subservient to Him.

'He knows all things infallibly' (1). The words of Isaiah again confirm the truth - "the Lord of hosts hath sworn, saying, Surely as I have thought, so shall it come to pass; and as I have purposed, so shall it stand" (Is. 14.24). Or again "I am God, and there is none like Me ... My counsel shall stand, and I will do all My pleasure" (Is. 46.9-10). This same God is still in control. His infallible counsel will still come to pass - nothing happens by chance - He is still on the throne!

He knows all things immutably. This is confirmed by the wise man in the book of Proverbs - "the counsel of the Lord, that shall stand" (19.21). Man's heart has 'many devices'. His counsel alters to suit changing circumstances. Not so the Divine counsel - it is immutable and dependable. Hence we should hear His counsel that "thou mayest be wise in thy latter end" (Prov. 19.20).

God is Sovereign

The omniscience of God is inextricably linked with His sovereignty. Without this attribute God could not be the rightful governor of the universe. The whole of creation would be out of control with no Fatherly and dynamic guidance. He is aware of what we need to eat, to drink and to wear! "Your heavenly Father knoweth that ye have need of all these things" (Mt. 6.32).

The final judgement is in His hands. He "will bring to light the hidden things of darkness, and will make manifest the counsels of the hearts" (1 Cor. 4.5). How glad we are that "God the Judge of all" (Heb. 12.23) will be on the throne then - nothing unknown to Him, everything perfectly balanced, no miscarriage of justice - the final verdict perfect! See Psalm 1.5-6. Justice cannot be exercised without omniscience.

God is Worthy of Worship

Worship is based on the worth of its object and the relative unworthiness of the worshipper. Surely omniscience is one of the great subjects which focuses our hearts on the worthiness of God. At the same time our corresponding unworthiness in view of our limited knowledge is immediately apparent. Being thus humbled in the presence of such a great God should produce an attitude of adoring wonder. And wonder inevitably leads to worship!

The omniscience of God is a subject too deep for human minds to fathom. But this very fact is another reason why a worshipful response should be the result. In fact the very essence of prayer is to bring our will into conformity with the Divine will. It is making His thoughts our thoughts. Thus this truth should produce a spirit of dependence on a God who knows! Indeed we pray because God does know - not to inform Him of something outwith His knowledge!

THE PRACTICAL IMPLICATIONS OF OMNISCIENCE - MANWARD

Again this aspect of the subject can be looked at in a variety of ways. It can be a real **challenge** but it can also be a real **comfort**. The challenge comes by appreciating that God knows our shortcomings; the comfort comes by appreciating that God knows our needs and "the way that we take".

The Challenge of the Subject

There is a perfection in God's knowledge that we can practically deny in a number of particulars. For example we may permit sin because man cannot see it all the while forgetting that God can. How can we fail to learn from the sad acts of David - not only in the case of Bathsheba but equally in the case of Uriah the Hittite? Was it hidden from the eye of man? - it was known to God! Little wonder when David's sin was made known to him he cried with bitter repentance, "Against Thee, Thee only, have I sinned, and done this evil in Thy sight" (Ps. 51.4). 'Secret sins are more against God than man'(1). We should remember that "He walketh in the circuit of heaven" (Job 22.14).

This perfection may also be denied in partial confessions of sins before God. Remember the case of Achan and Joshua's admonition to him? "Achan ... make confession unto Him ... hide it not" (Josh. 7.19). How searching - what a challenge! 'To drop out some fragments of confession ... is a plain denial ... of Divine knowledge'(1).

The challenge should not be lost in practical implications for assembly service. Does our worship spring from "feigned lips" (Ps. 17.1) - a contradiction between the heart and the tongue? Or is it from a full heart bubbling up with good matter - a result of our meditation? (Ps. 45.1 cst. Ps. 78.36). It is known to God! Do we cherish hypocritical pretences to exempt ourselves from Divine service? The whole is known to Him. We may deceive others - we cannot deceive God!

It is surely too a spur in gospel activity - a truth to challenge the sinner. There is no refuge in secrecy to a sinner - think of Adam, Jonah, Achan and Gehazi.

There is no shield in hypocrisy - think of Judas, Herod and the Pharisees. There is no diminishing of sin with the passing of time - think of Amalek (1Sam. 15.2) and Ephraim (Hos. 13.12). There is no appeal to miscarriage of justice - 'the eye of His knowledge directs the hand of His justice'(1). See Psalm 10.14.

THE COMFORT OF THE SUBJECT

It would be inappropriate to conclude without considering this important aspect of the subject. There is surely supreme comfort to God's people in the words of the Psalmist "He knoweth our frame; He remembereth that we are dust" (Ps. 103.14). The omniscient God is thus a fit object of trust. We can depend upon Him! He knows us! What a tragedy it would be if He were ignorant of our circumstances. But each one is known to Him who said "I am the good shepherd, and know my sheep, and am known of mine" (Jn. 10.14). We are all known intimately, known fully, known personally - "The Lord knoweth them that are His" (2 Tim. 2.19).

What shall we say of the secret sighs, the silent prayers, the unarticulated burdens, the broken hearts, the undeserved persecutions, the sore afflictions known among God's people? Their conditions are all known to an omniscient God. He hears, He understands, He cares. All the afflictions are known to Him. Is this not why the Book of the Psalms has been such an inspiration to God's people over the centuries and continues to be the resource of the afflicted?

This very perfection is also the basis of appeal of a devoted heart desirous of walking in the "way everlasting". "Search me, O God, and know my heart: try me and know my thoughts: and see if there be any wicked way in me, and lead me in the way everlasting" (Ps. 139.23-24). This Psalm as a whole deals with the subject of the omniscience of God in a remarkable way. Little wonder that David says "Such knowledge is too wonderful for me" (v.6). It is too wonderful for us as well but this very fact provides the basis upon which a devoted walk can be undertaken. Secret sins can be searched out not for punishment but for pardon! 'His omniscience stirs not up His justice to revenge, but His mercy to pity'(1).

What a comfort to know that such a God is our God! 'The consideration of this excellent perfection should make us to acquiesce in God and to rely upon Him in every circumstance of life'(1).

'There are two words of light Divine that fall upon this heart of mine,
That thrill me in the hour of gain, that still me in the hour of pain:
*Two words with wondrous power, sufficient unto any hour - **He knows.**'*

References

1. Charnock S. Discourses Upon the Existence and Attributes of God. Baker Book House 1979, ISBN 0-8010-2437-4. 11th printing, May 1993.

2. Hoste W. Studies in Bible Doctrines. John Ritchie Ltd., 1948.

3. Zodhiates S. The Complete Word Study Dictionary - New Testament. AMG Publishers Chatanooga, TN 37422, June 1992.

THE OMNIPRESENCE OF GOD

By Thomas Bentley

ITS MENTION:

Neither the word in its noun form 'omnipresence' nor in its adjectival form 'omnipresent' appears within the page of Scripture. It is, however, a word which conveys truth inherent in the Word of God as expressive of a Divine attribute that is essential to and an integral part of the God we know in Scripture. The fact that God is everywhere present is presupposed throughout the Bible and at times is definitively stated. God's omnipresence is contiguous to His omnipotence and omniscience. Seeing He is everywhere, He is able to express His power and exercise His prerogative, for there is never anything nor anyone beyond His cognizance anywhere.

ITS MEANING:

The conception of omnipresence comes to us through the revelation God has given of Himself. Sound doctrine has always affirmed the omnipresence of God and has proclaimed it as a vital particle of truth. Naturally, there are many speculative ideas about such a subject, but, just as it ought, the findings of the Word of God have far exceeded that of philosophy in any form. The all-pervading presence of the living God is one of the most essential realities, that commands our interest in both a perceptive and a practical measure.

Omnipresence represents to us the real and universal presence of God in all that God has revealed Himself to be - in the fulness of character and versatility of energy of which God is possessed. It is the present mode of being, by virtue of which all the moral worth of God is everywhere available. The Psalmist in this connection is a better guide than the philosopher can be. Psalm 139.7-12 gives a clear and a classical expression of the conviction that there is absolutely no possibility of putting a distance between a soul and God. Faith accepts without reservation and celebrates with rejoicing the real presence of The Eternal, in these words, "underneath are the everlasting arms" (Deut. 33.27).

Three aspects of truth appear as a result of the foregoing:-

God's Eternity - Ps. 90.2; 102.27; Isa. 41.4; 1 Tim. 1.17; Jude 25. The "I AM" of Ex. 3.14 involves eternity.

God's Immensity - 1 Kings 8.27; 2 Chr. 2.6; 6.18.

God's Ubiquity - Ps. 139.7; Jer. 23.23; Acts 17.27,28.

All that is attributable to God is attributable to the Lord Jesus, and of course to the Holy Spirit of God. Essential Godhead, in all its necessary and wondrously revealed aspects, finds its eternal existence and effectual expression in each Person of the Trinity. Therefore, omnipresence is a characteristic of the Spirit (Ps. 139.7). Paul's language in Philippians chapter two is familiar, when he speaks of the Lord Jesus as "being in the form of God." Seeing then that He never left that form, it is evident that in perfect manhood He possessed all the attributes essential to Godhead. It is true, that when He was "found in fashion as a man," and moved on earth as a man among men, speaking reverently, He was physically located in one place at a time. However, on reading the first chapter of John's Gospel, we hear the Saviour speak to Nathanael these words, "When thou wast under the fig tree I saw thee." To the worshipping heart, this bespeaks omnipresence. Then in chapter four, the Lord Jesus is in Cana of Galilee, yet He heals the nobleman's son who was sick in Capernaum. It is evident then, that even when in manhood's low estate, the Saviour overcame all limitation either by time or space.

ITS MANNER:

When we affirm the omnipresence of God we establish beyond question the fact that God is above all limitations of space, and can accomplish everywhere all He can do anywhere. All that He is in Himself as God, is everywhere at hand for any act He wishes to perform. He never needs to move in order to reach a position or place in which He chooses to operate. The God who acts according to His own will, wherever He chooses is God omnipresent. Just how His power and energy go forth from Him, is beyond us either to explain or describe, but we know that from Him they issue forth everywhere unhindered and unlimited. Human language is obviously limited as is our scanty thought, yet we need not be troubled if we cannot say much more than this about the manner of His omnipresence, for surely the conception we have grasped is clear, convincing and comforting. Even though we cannot actually picture such a presence because of our finite comprehension, one thing is perfectly true, a personal consciousness of it is possible and precious in the soul without a mental picture. It is recorded that one day an atheist wrote on his daughter's school pad the expression, God is Nowhere. On asking the child to read it, she read: 'God is Now Here.' Apparently the father was melted to tears as his unbelief gave way to trust in the God who is everywhere. Before moving on to other aspects of our subject, we must state categorically that omnipresence is expressive not merely of God's power and of His will, but essentially of His Being.

The Scriptures speak anthropomorphically of God relative to His movements. We read "... the Lord thy God walketh," while other passages speak of His "eyes," "voice," "feet," "hands," suggesting a corporeal God.

Though these terms appear frequently, we know from the ministry of the Lord Jesus that, God is spirit (Jn. 4.24 RV). The writers who used these terms never conceived of God being circumscribed by space. The Theophanic appearances are not intended to disclose what God is in the nature of His being, but simply how he condescends to accomplish His work for His People. It stamps a redemptive and revelatory purpose in each area and on every occasion, which does not, in the mind of the writer, conflict with divine omnipresence. The patriarchs were conscious of God's presence as from place to place they erected altars and called upon the name of the Lord. Jacob expressively confirms, "The Lord is in this place" and later avows "If God will be with me" (Gen. 28.16-20). By this we recognise they gave expression that what was embodied in them was not a conception of a locally circumscribed Deity, but the increasing and assuring consciousness of the gracious presence of God wherever they went.

Then God is said to dwell in the Tabernacle (Ex. 25.8), on Mt. Zion (Ps. 3.4; 99.1-2), in the Temple (Ps. 20.2; 26.8; 46.4-5). This leads us on to the truth expressed by John "The Word became flesh and dwelt among us." He who is essentially and eternally God manifests His presence in a form visible, tangible and audible as again John confirms in 1 John 1.1-3. Through the incoming of the Holy Spirit, yet another consciousness of the Presence is known in the church which is His body (Eph. 2.21-22) and in the individual believer (Rom. 5.5) and also in the local church (1 Tim. 3.15). Neither is there any incongruity as the eternal state is reached, when the Presence is known and displayed forever in total conformity to eternal purpose (Rev. 21.3). Therefore the manifold manner of the Presence is enthralling, entrancing and enduring.

ITS MESSAGE:

Like every other facet of truth, omnipresence has its effective message with practical consequences for all who embrace its reality. The runaway Hagar when made conscious of this truth confessed, "Thou God seest me" (Gen. 16.13). Though the message was comforting it also proved commanding for she was directed to return to her mistress. Even though in extenuating circumstances, the impact of the truth had effectual power, she obeyed complacently. Nathanael bowed in confession of all that the Son of God is, when he was brought to realise the omnipresence of the Lord. Likely he went under the fig tree so as to be out of the sight of everyone, that he might mediate upon the Word. Was he reading Genesis 16 that day? Somehow I believe he was. When he was told by the Lord Jesus, "When thou wast under the fig tree I saw thee," the ensuing result was confession and adoration. Though the eye of man may not be upon me, I must remember I am never out of the range of His ever present, perceptive eye. How preservative a power this should prove to be in our daily living. To the Psalmist it was not only a sober reality, but also a source of rejoicing to realise he could never reach a place where he would be outside the range of His presence. (Ps. 139.7-12). Yet it is with equal awe and gladness he celebrates God's omnipresence as a fact inevitable and as a force invaluable, stimulating his confidence in the God whom he trusts. Jonah seemingly either became insensitive to truth or else totally insubordinate to it, when he tried to flee from the presence of the Lord (Jonah 1.3). The consequences stand as a message to all who would be so disposed as to attempt the inevitable.

ITS MERCY:

God's saints throughout the ages have experienced in their Sorrow

THE COMFORT THE PRESENCE IMPARTS

The People of God have drawn immense comfort from these words, "When thou passest through the waters, I will be with thee" (Isa. 43.2). The truth of His omnipresence becomes ever so precious in our Solitude when we hear Him say, "I will never leave thee, nor forsake thee" (Heb. 13.5).

Let us enter experimentally into the truth of His omnipresence that in our Service we may face

THE CHALLENGE THE PRESENCE IMPELS

The risen Saviour would rekindle fresh devotion in service when on resurrection He commissioned His Own and said by way of assurance, "Lo I am with you alway" (Matt. 28.20). It would nerve us to greater endeavour in pursuit of the interests of the Kingdom to fulfil in detail His commands.

Surely in our daily walk this truth will affect our Sojourn by

THE CONSTRAINT THE PRESENCE IMPOSES

Would we ever wish to follow the defiance of Cain when he "Went out from the presence of the Lord?" May we never imitate the disobedience of Jonah when he paid the price to flee "from the presence of the Lord."

ITS MARVEL:

IT PRODUCES ADORATION - Isaiah 6.1-13

Isaiah's encounter with the God of Israel, the Lord of hosts, exhibits the truth of omnipresence in most acceptable forms. He is conscious of the Lord sitting upon a throne, high and lifted up. Then he observes that His train (skirts) fills the temple, and on hearing the song of the seraphim, he is assured that "the whole earth is full of His glory." Clearly it all comes within the scope of the Prophet's theology, for he apprehends the sense of divine omnipresence without difficulty and accepts it without doubt. His resultant response to the call of the Lord bespeaks his adorative appreciation of the God who called.

IT PROMOTES AWARENESS - Isaiah 8.16-18

The section in which chapter 8 is found mentions Immanuel. Chapter 7 Immanuel's Descent; chapter 8 Immanuel's Doctrine; chapter 9 Immanuel's Deity; chapter 10 Immanuel's Dependence; chapter 11 Immanuel's Dominion. The short selected section (8.16-18) carries the interpretation of Immanuel, "God is with us." When pressure mounts against the testimony of God, it is comforting to have this assurance that, (1) Numbers will not avail, (2) Arms will not avail, (3) Counsel will not avail, (4) Words will not avail. Why? Because God is with us. What comfort and consolation an awareness of the Presence ministers.

IT PREVENTS APATHY - Isaiah 26.1-10

In these verses the Prophet speaks of those things that are the product of His Presence: (1).Security (2).Tranquillity (3).Humility (4).Integrity (5).Fidelity (6).Majesty. All supineness and dispassion totally disappear when the presence of God is fully realised. Coldness and frigidity give place to warmth and fervour as God is consciously known among His People. Heart aspiration is fully met by the fulness of God's presence, promoting diligence, devotion and delight.

May it please God to make every reader of these lines familiar with the 'Practice of the Presence.'

THE IMMUTABILITY OF GOD

By A W Foster

Among the perfections which characterise our God, distinguishing Him from His creatures, none is of greater comfort to His saints than His immutability. The dictionary definition of the word "immutability" is "unchangeableness" and in applying such to God, it must be appreciated that this quality belongs to Him eternally. Being creatures of time we are given to change as we grow and mature, and outside influences, whether good or bad, bear upon us and all too often we show ourselves to be quite fickle. But God, being eternal, stands outside of time altogether and is unmoved by any and all influences and happenings. Indeed were it to be otherwise He would cease to be the Almighty God to whom is heard addressed a glorious song of worship by a multitude of voices in the courts of heaven "saying, Hallelujah: for the Lord our God, the Almighty, reigneth" (Rev. 19.6 RV).

How good, how very reassuring it is to know that the One to whom we turned in faith for salvation, upon whom we rely day by day for guidance and protection and in whom all our hopes for the future reside is not only unchanging but unchangeable. "I am the Lord," He declared of old through His servant Malachi, "I change not" (Mal. 3.6), thereby revealing that His abiding steadfastness is a necessary consequence of Him being Lord. This fact becomes even clearer to us when we observe that the name "Lord" which He here uses, is His lovely name of "Jehovah" which signifies 'He that always was, that always is, and that ever is to come' (Thomas Newberry). His immutability is therefore an expression of His eternity of being, and the rich blessedness which was the enjoyed portion of Israel and of which Moses did speak so movingly in his final benediction upon them, is beautifully expressed in his words, "The eternal God is thy refuge, and underneath are the everlasting arms". Small wonder he then proceeded to exclaim, "Happy art thou, O Israel" (Deut. 33.27,29). Would we deny to the saints of today the reassurance conveyed in that choice blessing, knowing as we do that same eternal God as our Father and being like them, a "people saved by the Lord"?

The full significance of the name "Jehovah" was not made known to the early patriarchs and it is only when we come to Exodus 3 that we find the Lord fully revealing Himself to His people as such, something which He later explains in Exodus 6. The setting is striking as, in response to the cry of His people by reason of their sore afflictions, He appears to Moses at Horeb from the midst of the burning bush, pledging Himself as about to redeem His people from "the hand of the Egyptians". Its deep meaningfulness is there revealed to us as Moses, somewhat anxiously, seeks from the Lord an appropriate name for him to take to the people and we read "God said unto Moses, 'I AM THAT I AM' ... Thus shalt thou say unto the children of Israel, 'The Lord God of your fathers ... hath sent me unto you' ... This is my name for ever" (Ex. 3.14,15). What comfort, what encouragement this name ought to have ministered to Israel in their distressing circumstances as they were thus reminded that their Deliverer was the "I AM" - Jehovah, the immutable One, "the Lord God of their fathers"! Forty years later, as the life of that remarkable man of God reaches to a fitting, if premature, climax upon the banks of the River Jordan, with the promised land within their sight he summons the nation to him and shares with them the glorious song which he had composed for the occasion, a song which is at once historical and prophetical in its content. Dramatically he calls upon the heavens and the earth to give heed "because" he declares, "I will publish the name of the Lord", and so very appropriately it is His name "Jehovah" that he there proclaims, then proceeds in memorable language to exhort the gathered tribes to join with him in praising the Lord. "Ascribe ye greatness unto our God" he cries, "He is the Rock, His work is perfect ..." (Deut. 32.3,4). How wonderfully that title of "the Rock" brings into prominence the immutability, the unchangeableness, of the Lord. That failure had dogged their steps throughout their wilderness wanderings is acknowledged by Moses in his song wherein he describes them as "a perverse and crooked generation" in spite of which the Lord has remained constant. Truly He is uniquely and emphatically "the Rock" being so described five times over in the song and frequently in other parts of Scripture, and if you refer to the Revised Version of Deuteronomy 32 you will discover that these words "The Rock" are really the title to the song! The metaphor of the rock plainly represents God's abiding faithfulness and constancy of purpose, with Moses proceeding to describe Him in the song as "a God of faithfulness and without iniquity" where the word "faithfulness" signifies "firmness" or "steadfastness". Thus does Moses rejoice in the name of the Lord, "The Rock ... a God of steadfastness ..."!

But Moses didn't only compose songs of triumph, for you will recall that he penned that very touching 90th Psalm in which he reviews the sad history of man and speaks of the brevity of each of our lives, observing in verse 10 that our "strength ... is soon cut off, and we fly away". But the Psalm is entitled "a prayer" within which we find Moses expressing his absolute confidence in the everlasting God, and at the very outset he is heard acknowledging such, declaring "Before the mountains were brought forth, or ever thou hadst formed the earth and the world, even from everlasting to everlasting, Thou art God." The hymn writer has captured something of this same contrast between us and our God when he penned the familiar lines,

'Change and decay in all around I see:
O Thou who changest not, abide with me.'

I pause and reflect that many years later the Lord had to lament over that highly favoured people, "I remember thee ... the love of thine espousals" then adding sorrowfully, "they are gone far from Me" (Jer. 2.2,5). Alas how little loyalty was to be found in them, how prone they were to stray, how flighty they were in their affections! Nor think for one minute that we today are immune from such backsliding. In the early days of church history, no company of saints can be found more highly favoured than that in Ephesus, yet of those privileged saints no less we hear the Lord express His sorrowful lament, "thou hast left thy first love" (Rev. 2.4). But He is not so! He does not change, nay He cannot change, abiding perpetually the same. He who "in the beginning ... created the heavens and the earth" (Gen. 1.1 JND), is the same who came unto Moses in a dense cloud and thundered at Sinai, is the same who withdrew into the awesome darkness of Golgotha and is the same who one day will pronounce from His throne, "Behold, I make all things new" (Rev. 21.5). So to the straying "families of Israel" He declares through that self-same prophet Jeremiah, "Yea, I have loved thee with an everlasting love ... again I will build thee ... and My people shall be satisfied with My goodness, saith the Lord" (Jer. 31.3,4,14). Oh to revel in the appreciation of His immutability - "I am the Lord, I change not"!

Other psalmists too caught the thrill of this encouraging truth and are heard on several occasions expressing their confident trust in the Lord as "the Rock". For example we find the Psalmist David so exulting no less than four times over in Psalm 18, beginning the psalm by expressing his deep affection for the Lord in the words, "I will love Thee, O Lord, my strength", then continuing "The Lord is my rock, and my fortress, and my deliverer; My God, my rock, in whom I will trust" (Ps. 18.1,2 Newberry margin). In another psalm we are privileged to hear David at prayer and again we find him expressing his deep confidence in the Lord as "the Rock", crying out from the depths of his soul "When my heart is overwhelmed: Lead me to the Rock that is higher than I. For Thou hast been a shelter for me, and a strong tower ..." (Ps. 61.2,3). Down through succeeding generations many among the saints have echoed the self-same sentiments when experiencing adversity, and how we all love to join so heartily in singing the familiar words of another old hymn,

'The Lord's our Rock, in Him we hide:
A shelter in the time of storm!
Secure whatever ill betide:
A shelter in the time of storm!'

This concept of the Lord as "the Rock" should gladden all our hearts and have us continually buoyed-up in spirit, realising that it is a tacit acknowledgement of His immutability!

But let us return for a moment to Malachi 3. "I am the Lord" we heard Him there assert, "I change not" then significantly He adds "therefore ye sons of Jacob are not consumed." His description of them as "sons of Jacob" is surely a poignant reminder to them of their frequent tendency to stray and He would thus remind them that their very survival, never mind their assured and glorious future, is but a reflection of His unchangeableness and in spite of their endemic waywardness.

The Book of Nehemiah provides us with the historical account of those days when Malachi exercised his prophetic ministry. What a fascinating glimpse we are given in chapter 9 therein of the returned remnant of the nation as they assemble before the Lord in Jerusalem and after separating themselves from the strangers who were there and listening to the reading of the Word of God prompting confession and worship, they then are exhorted by the Levites in this fashion, "Stand up and bless the Lord your God from everlasting to everlasting" (Neh. 9.5 RV), a call which is followed by a detailed review of God's abiding faithfulness towards them throughout their history to date, climaxing in their grateful admission, "Thou art a gracious and merciful God ... who keepest covenant and mercy" (Neh. 9.31,32). How spiritually intelligent those godly Levites showed themselves to be in so exhorting the people that day, and how well they understood the immutability of their God!

Even the mercenary prophet Balaam recognised this same blessed truth. We direct our minds to his shameful attempts to secure "the wages of unrighteousness" from Balak, king of the Moabites, yet finding himself repeatedly being prevented from so doing by the Lord, and most amazingly being used by Him as the vehicle for communicating some remarkable prophecies. Listen afresh to the words which the Lord put into the prophet's mouth as he stood on the top of Mount Pisgah, words which he then conveyed to Balak in a parable. "God is not a man, that He should lie; neither a son of man, that He should repent: Shall He say and not do? And shall He speak and not make it good?" (Num. 23.19 JND). How frustrating such words must have been, both to the king and to the prophet, but how wonderfully reassuring to Israel. In spite of the repeated attempts of the Moabite king to bring about their downfall, the Lord remained firm in His avowed intention to bless them. Because God is immutable, His word is therefore irreversible and not one of His promises can be changed or fail. We do well in applying such words of assurance to ourselves, remembering the words of the apostle to the saints at Corinth when he reaffirmed the abiding faithfulness of God in keeping all His promises to the last letter, "all the promises of God in Him (i.e. in Christ) are yea, and in Him Amen" (2 Cor. 1.20).

We must however consider very carefully two clear implications of this inspired parable from the lips of Balaam, as recorded in Numbers 23.19. Firstly he distinctly asserts that God cannot repent. Said Balaam, "Hath He said, and shall He not do it? Or hath He spoken, and shall He not make it good?" and again, "God is not a man ... neither a son of man, that He should repent" (JND). Have we not been emphasizing this blessed truth in our present study and is such not an integral element of His immutability? Yet as our minds range over the Scriptures, we meet with apparent contradictions of this truth as on several occasions we do actually read of God repenting. For example, we read of Him so doing in the days of Noah when confronted by the rampant upsurge in wickedness on the part of His creature man (Gen. 6.6); again we read similarly in the days of the judges because of the oppression of His people at the hand of their enemies (Judg. 2.18); then again in the reign of Saul we find that His faithful servant Samuel was deeply grieved and "cried unto the Lord all night" when He revealed to him that He had repented of establishing Saul as king, "for he ... hath not performed My commandments" He declared (1 Sam. 15.11); and even in the days of Jonah, in response to the repentance of the people of Nineveh, we are told that "God repented of the evil, that He had said that He would do unto them" (Jonah 3.10). O let me hasten to emphasize that these all are but apparent contradictions for there is none such to be found anywhere in Scripture far less in the actions of the Lord. It is therefore certain that, however we interpret these references to God repenting, we cannot understand them to signify that He ever changes His mind or that He can be persuaded by circumstances to deviate from His eternal counsels. The 19th century Pusey aptly, if somewhat quaintly commented, 'change implies imperfection: it changes to that which is either more perfect or less perfect: to somewhat which that being, who changes, is not or has not. But God has everything in Himself perfectly.' Now read that quotation a second time and you will better appreciate just how truly apt it is!

The comments made by James, after the somewhat acrimonious discussion which took place among the early Christians in Jerusalem over the issue of circumcision, as he responded to what Peter and Barnabas and Paul had recounted to them, are apposite to our study. Said he - and I judge manifestly under the Spirit's leading - "Known unto God are all His works from the beginning of the world" (Acts 15.18), with Mr Darby translating "known from eternity". God cannot be taken by surprise nor caught-out by events. How are we then to rightly interpret these references to Him repenting? I submit that we are not evading the problem by suggesting that in so unmasking His deep emotions and speaking of Himself as grieving and as repenting, God is accommodating Himself to us in order to make Himself thereby understood by our finite comprehension. There is not so much as an inference in any of these passages that God was confronted with an unforeseen contingency, but rather He so expresses Himself in order to emphatically express His abhorrence of man's sinful and stubbornly rebellious ways. Samuel makes this abundantly plain with regard to God's rejection of Saul as king, when he quite categorically says to the rejected king, "the Strength of Israel will not lie nor repent: for He is not a man that He should repent" (1 Sam. 15.29), while it is clearly evident in Genesis 6 that God is not even so much as implying that He had made a mistake in creating man but rather that He was changing His actions towards men, resulting from their stubborn rebellion towards Him and their precipitate preoccupation with evil. We therefore must conclude that when we read of God repenting, we must not, we dare not, attribute to Him any action which contradicts His absolute omniscience nor see in Him a reaction which is contrary to His eternal counsels, remembering that He "worketh all things after the counsel of His own will:" and that with Him there "is no variableness, neither shadow of turning" (Eph. 1.11; Jas. 1.17).

But there is something else in Balaam's parable which we must also consider. I refer to his reference to God not being a man, nor a son of man. Of course such is perfectly true, yet as we turn to our New Testament scriptures, we are confronted by what is there described as a "mystery", a matter hitherto not made known and one moreover, not discernible by the natural man viz., that "God has been manifested in flesh" (1 Tim. 3.16 JND). How could we possibly comprehend such truth without having the indwelling Holy Spirit as our teacher? "But ye have an unction from the Holy one" John explains, "and ye know all things" (1 Jn. 2.20). O wonder of all wonders as, without ceasing to be God, He "became flesh and dwelt among us" (Jn. 1.14 JND), delighting on numerous occasions to describe Himself as "the Son of man". We must therefore now turn and explore God's immutability within the context of the incarnation.

No more blessed nor more rewarding occupation can be found for the child of God than the contemplation of the person of our Lord Jesus. Whether we follow His footsteps here below as traced out for us by the Spirit of God in the four Gospels, or search out the manifold glories of His character as unfolded in the Epistles or delve into the final unveiling of His eternal worth as found displayed in the Book of the Revelation, we but discover our confidence in the immutability of our God deepened. Twice over in the Epistle to the Hebrews we are exhorted to consider Him, and as we respond to that appeal and consider the exposition of His blessed person as given within that very Epistle, we find His immutability clearly and quite emphatically taught. We gasp as we see His mighty stoop vividly described for us in chapter 2 as, being "made a little lower than the angels", He partakes of flesh and blood, and taking hold of the seed of Abraham, He is "made like unto His brethren", the closing verse disclosing that "He himself hath suffered being tempted." Well might the apostle Paul elsewhere exclaim, "ye know the grace of our Lord Jesus Christ ... He became poor" (2 Cor. 8.9). Yet ere we read such a disclosure of His stupendous stoop, we find ourselves in the opening chapter of Hebrews being confronted by a choice exposition of His solitary and eternal glory as the Son of God. Seven quotations from the scriptures of old are there presented to us which combine to affirm His absolute superiority over the angels of heaven and over the creation from His hand, among which we find, in vv.10-12, one from Psalm 102 setting forth the vivid contrast between the Creator and His creation. The psalmist describes to us a doomed creation - "they shall perish", in contrast to which he asserts, "but Thou continuest" (Westcott). Being subject to time and to decay "they shall be changed" he further muses, then exclaims in delight, "but Thou art the same"! And when we eventually reach to the closing chapter of the epistle we find it suitably rounded-off with a further clear and emphatic declaration of His unchangeableness in the familiar words, "Jesus Christ the same yesterday, and today, and for ever" (Heb. 13.8). In the setting of the opening chapter, He is being hailed as God as we read, "unto the Son He saith, 'Thy throne, O God, is for ever and ever ...'" (v.8), while in the closing chapter, the title "Jesus Christ" is used, a title which belongs to Him in His humanity, albeit now ascended to glory. Thus we find it plainly taught that both as God and as man, He abides "the same", He cannot, He does not, He will not change - He is immutable. We look around us at creation and assume the permanence of the towering mountains and the ethereal skies, but "they shall perish" the psalmist testifies, "they all shall wax old as doth a garment ... they shall be changed" in contrast to which he affirms of the Son, "Thou remainest ... Thou art the same!" 'Change with us is constant, universal. How unspeakably blessed that the Christ to whom we have transferred our life and hopes is the same unto the ages, yesterday and today and forever' (Wm R Newell). The words of another Psalm readily spring to mind, "Great is the Lord, and greatly to be praised ... for this God is our God for ever and ever" (Ps. 48.1,14). We do well to observe the setting of the writer's assertion of the unchangeableness of Christ in Hebrews 13, for in verse 9 he advances such as a valid reason for our not being swept about by the winds of strange teachings. He remains our only, our sure, our immovable foundation.

What about the days when He was found dwelling among men? We turn and peruse the early chapters of Luke's Gospel and there witness the growth and development of the child Jesus. Here it is we read that "the child grew and waxed strong in spirit, filled with wisdom ...", and again that "Jesus increased in wisdom and stature..." (Lk. 2.40,52). Do such statements even so much as imply that He changed in any way with the growth which was taking place in His physical and intellectual development, that He matured in the way that we do and by reason of such modified His thinking as He grew older? Never! We banish all such thoughts from our minds, together with the apocryphal notions of a child prodigy, and bow in wonder which leads to worship as we view "the Mighty God, the Father of eternity" (Is. 9.6 Newberry margin), "being found in fashion as a man" (Phil. 2.8), growing and developing unfettered, untarnished by sin - perfect man and perfect God. How fittingly we find Luke prefacing his account of the public ministry of the perfect man with the story of His baptism when "the heaven was opened ... and a voice came from heaven, which said, 'Thou art My beloved Son ...'" (Lk. 3.21,22). Alongside Luke's account of the perfect man we place John's record of the Son of God, recalling his choice introductory description of Him as the eternal Word. How appropriate, how accurate a title for the One who abides unchangeable, and as he sets forth his brief description of the incarnation, John expresses it in terms quite unambiguous, "the Word" he writes, "became flesh ..." (Jn. 1.14 JND) thereby revealing that the One who trod this scene of time as the Son of man, was the immutable, the unchangeable Word! How fitting too that we find in his opening chapter, the forerunner John describing himself as but "a voice", a voice being only a vehicle to communicate that which is embodied in a word. But Christ is not but a voice, for He who came forth to make God known is emphatically the absolute, the abiding, the changeless "Word", whose "name is called, 'The Word of God'" (Rev 19.13)! Well do we sing the choice sentiments,

'Thou art the Everlasting Word,
The Father's only Son,
God manifestly seen and heard,
And heaven's belovèd One.
In Thee, most perfectly expressed,
The Father's glories shine,
Of the full Deity possessed,
Eternally divine.'

How fitting then, as we peruse the record of this fourth Gospel, to find here the Lord applying to His own person that incommunicable name of God to which we have already made reference, declaring to the Jews as they debated with Him, "Verily, verily, I say unto you, Before Abraham was, I am" (Jn. 8.58). Do appreciate the full extent of the contrast He is making by these words. Abraham was but a man with a beginning, whereas the Lord Jesus stands outside of time altogether as the eternally constant "I am", timeless in His existence and absolute in His essence! Tragically they failed to recognise in the One who stood before them that day, the very One who had said to their fathers through Moses, "I am come down to deliver ... I AM that I AM" (Ex. 3.8,14). Again He has - in person and in wondrous grace - "come down to deliver". Jehovah, the Saviour of their fathers, stands in their very midst and their only response is to pick up stones and angrily hurl them at Him.

But the coming of Christ to dwell among men was outstandingly with a view to "the suffering of death" (Heb. 2.9) and His departure from the temple that day as they were about to stone Him, led to the choice unfolding of His essential work as "the Good Shepherd" who "giveth His life for the sheep" (Jn. 10.11). His death accomplished at Calvary is the pivot of our faith and the means whereby we have been reconciled to God, yet we must fully understand that the cross has not changed God in Himself nor in His dealings with man. There was no need for Him to be reconciled to us, but in His eternal love He has provided the means for us to be reconciled to Him. He who said to Israel at the giving of the Law, "I the Lord thy God am a jealous God ..." (Ex. 20.5), is the same whom the apostle did describe as the "God, who is rich in mercy ..." coming out in wondrous grace to bestow salvation upon guilty sinners. That which makes the difference for us is our being found "in Christ" as we "who sometimes were far off are made nigh by the blood of Christ" (Eph. 2.4,13). Earlier in that choice epistle we have confirmed to us that such blessings are ours as those "chosen in Him before the foundation of the world ... according to the purpose of Him who worketh all things after the counsel of His own will" (Eph. 1.4,11) and we could well echo the sentiments expressed in the Epistle to the Hebrews where we read of "the immutability of His counsel." The cross and its effects upon our relationship with God do not reflect any change on His part but rather confirm the abiding significance of His name Jehovah as proclaimed by Himself at Sinai, "The Lord, The Lord God, merciful and gracious ..." (Ex. 34.6).

We direct our minds to the final book in the sacred canon, "The Revelation of Jesus Christ" and to our delight discover that it commences with His majestic declaration, "'I am Alpha and Omega, the beginning and the ending,' saith the Lord, 'which is, and which was, and which is to come, the Almighty'" (Rev. 1.1, 8). In the Newberry Reference Bible we find a footnote here suggesting that the words, "which is, and which was, and which is to come" correspond with the Hebrew name Jehovah and signify, "which always is, which ever was, and which always is the coming One". At least three times over we find this echo of His Jehovah name appearing in this Book of the Revelation, a striking reminder to us that He abides unchangeably the same. He who in the beginning brought worlds into being by a spoken word is the very One who will one day usher in a new heaven and a new earth as He makes "all things new". That He "always is" witnesses to His eternally abiding character, standing as He does outside of time itself and timeless in Himself; That He "always was" eloquently reminds us that no matter how far back we may probe in history, He pre-dates it all; That He "always is the coming One" projects our minds off to the ages to come and still we find Him there ahead of us as "the Coming One"! And then, across this majestic reminder of His underived and unchanging existence is heard His description of Himself as "the Almighty", a title to be found nine times over in this engrossing book, bearing witness to the omnipotent power which He possesses and to the sustaining resources which are ever available to us in Him. 'He is almighty in sustaining His people, yet equally almighty in judgment on His enemies' (Walter Scott). We turn to its closing verses and there find His repeated promise to return and His reminder, "I am Alpha and Omega, the beginning and the end, the first and the last" (Rev. 22.13). However we understand these choice titles which He employs, surely they combine to reaffirm our absolute confidence in His immutability.

In days of declining stability within society at large and rapidly accelerating changes taking place among God's people, may it be that our meditation together upon God's immutability will strengthen our faith and encourage us in the sure knowledge that He abides perpetually the same. "Rejoice in the Lord, O ye righteous ... The Lord bringeth the counsel of the nations to nought: He maketh the thoughts of the peoples to be of none effect. The counsel of the Lord standeth fast for ever, the thoughts of His heart to all generations. (Ps. 33.1,10,11 RV).

THE OMNIPOTENCE OF GOD

By Edward Griffiths

The omnipotence of God is a subject we do well to approach as Moses and Joshua when confronted by Divine Beings - with unshod feet, "for the place whereon thou standest is holy ground."

What we know of God, let alone the attributes of Deity, we owe to His graciousness and remarkable desire to be known by us. For "He dwelleth in the light which no man can approach unto; whom no man hath seen, nor can see: to whom be honour and power everlasting. Amen." (1 Tim. 6.16). The revealing of Himself has been in keeping with Hebrews 1.1,2, "at sundry times and in divers manners ... in these last days ... by His Son." Without such communications we would have had to confess like Agur, "I neither learned wisdom, nor have the knowledge of the Holy." (Prov. 30.3).

'The key to the understanding of the biblical doctrine of God is the name,' states B.W. Anderson. This statement is clearly the result of examining the Scriptures, the written revelation of God, which with discernment use the names and titles by which He is pleased to be known and are expressive of His nature and character and even of His presence - 1 Kings 8.29 reads, "My name shall be there," - let alone His power. 'The divine names receive and reflect scattered rays of heavenly truth as men can bear their effulgence; and when they have been set in our spiritual firmament they burn for ever. Thus each name authoritatively given to God is, so as to speak, a fresh and lasting revelation of His nature.' (Westcott). No one gave God His names. He chose them. Some people are remarkably named before birth - He alone chose His own names as One who had no "beginning of days."

So in Genesis 1.1 we learn of Elohim. A name God used as the Being who is plural, but acts as One, creating. 'A name expressive of Him being the Supreme Object of worship, the Adorable One', writes Newberry. Progression in revelation through the disclosure of His names is clearly designed as disclosed in Exodus 6.2-3, where it is recorded, "God spake unto Moses, and said unto him, I am the Lord (Jehovah); and I appeared unto Abraham, unto Isaac, and unto Jacob by the name of God Almighty, but by My name Jehovah was I not known to them." Hence in moving from Genesis 1.1 to Genesis 2.4 we find Elohim calls Himself, Jehovah Elohim i.e. the Supreme One to be worshipped is the Ever-Existent One, in the days when the heavens and the earth were made. Moving on to Genesis 4.1 and the expression of Eve at the birth of Cain we have the first occurrence of the name Jehovah being used alone. Then in Genesis 14.18, Melchizedek is referred to as the priest of El, i.e. the Most High God, possessor of heaven and earth. Here God presents Himself as the Mighty One. Newberry says of this title, 'It is generally connected with some one or more of the divine attributes.' The first example occurs in Genesis 17.1 as El Shaddai, meaning God All Sufficient or God Almighty. Hence at the outset of the Scriptures we are taught that our God is the Omnipotent One, and as such has the power to do anything consistent with His will and character, but, "He cannot deny Himself," nor can He lie. His omnipotence cannot be divorced from His absolute holiness and wisdom. How different from man, who, given some power for a lengthy period of time, is corrupted.

The Psalmist states, "Power belongeth unto God," (Ps. 62.11), i.e. in its fulness, variety and strength, and that eternally, since Paul wrote of "His eternal power and Godhead" (Rom. 1.20) or "Divinity" (JND). The divine attributes, like God, are eternal. For of God we read, "Even from everlasting to everlasting, Thou art God" (Ps. 90.2). Else there is development and progression within God, and that entails being now what He was not in the past i.e. in the past or now there were or are deficiencies, immaturities, imperfections and limitations. This cannot be considered for one moment. Whereas the attributes of God are characteristics or qualities which belong to His Person as distinct from His Person, each attribute of God, like God Himself is infinite. Hence His power is infinite, almighty power, both as to time and extent. In the case of power, God not only possesses it, but is power in as much as one of His names is Power, see Mark 14.62, "Ye shall see the Son of Man sitting on the right hand of Power, and coming in the clouds of heaven."

The word omnipotent occurs once only in the Authorised Version, in Revelation 19.6 where we read, "Alleluia: for the Lord God Omnipotent reigneth." (It is His manifest reign not His omnipotence that was just about to begin). Both omnipotence and sovereignty, closely allied concepts, like Himself are essentially eternal in relation to God.

The word omnipotence is of Latin derivation, and means, 'having all power.' As already shown, El Shaddai means God Almighty. The word almighty is an Anglo-Saxon word of the same meaning as omnipotent and is reserved in Scripture for God alone. Both omnipotent and almighty are words used to translate the one Greek word PANTOKRATOR (3841) meaning almighty or ruler of all. (Vine). Outside of the book of Revelation, the word is used once, in 2 Corinthians 6.18.

An understanding of the words helps us to appreciate the Psalmist, who in deep contemplation asked, "Who in the heaven can be compared unto the Lord? who among the sons of the mighty can be likened unto the Lord?" (Ps. 89.6) and the Gentile monarch Nebuchadnezzar, who after his most unusual experience at the hand of God, said, "All the inhabitants of the earth are reputed as nothing: and He doeth according to His will in the army of heaven, and among the inhabitants of the earth: and none can stay His hand or say unto Him, What doest Thou?" (Dan. 4.35).

It is not surprising that God's indignation was against Israel in Psalm 78.19 for, "They spake against God; they said, Can God ... ?" which is ignorance and insolence in the extreme. Yet amazingly, as will be shown later, the disciples of our Lord were guilty of asking a similar question despite being daily witnesses to His "mighty deeds."

Having touched upon God's omnipotence generally, it will be advantageous to witness it as manifest more particularly, in creation, in His dealings with the nations, with the Jews, in the church and finally in Christ. Care will need to be taken to ensure that the familiar language quoted does not detract or minimise the unfamiliar power God exercises in relation to each.

CREATION

In creation's process, product and perpetuation we have outstanding, knee-bending revelations of the omnipotence of God, as Job in particular experienced.

'This most eloquent system of sun, planets and comets, could only arise from the purpose and sovereignty of an intelligent and mighty being ... He rules them all, not as a soul of the world, but as sovereign Lord of all.' (Isaac Newton).

Unequivocally and succinctly the sacred volume begins, "In the beginning God created the heaven and the earth." (Gen. 1.1) - without material or manufacture. "He spake, and it was done; He commanded, and it stood fast." (Ps. 33.9). Human intelligence cannot grasp the enormity of the inherent power of God so displayed. It is, "Through faith we understand that the worlds were framed by the word of God, so that things which are seen were not made of things which do appear." (Heb. 11.3).

Creation is an object lesson to help us to begin to understand something of the nature and greatness of our God. "For the invisible things of Him from the creation of the world are clearly seen, being understood by the things that are made, even His eternal power and Godhead" (Rom. 1.20). The design, construction, function and preservation of creation entail awesome, breathtaking, humbling experiences for us, as we behold His omnipotence.

> 'Man is one form of life on the thin crust of a planet revolving around

> the sun ... an apparently minor star at the edge of the Milky Way. A multi-million starred galaxy, the Milky Way itself is only one among a million other galaxies moving in the infinity of space where traditional concepts of north and south are meaningless. 'It is a vision that dwarfs our globe and makes man seem very small. ... Despite their comparative smallness and the enormous distances of empty space that separate the planets in the solar family, the sun keeps its planets under strict control. ... The earth, ninety three million miles from the sun takes one year to complete its orbit, travelling at 66,600 miles per hour ... So tremendous is the radiation rate of the sun's energy that it loses four million tons in weight every second. Yet it is estimated that at that rate the sun could survive as the source of energy for at least another 8,000 million years.'
>
> (Editors of the Readers Digest Great World Atlas).

Little wonder that Scripture calls our God, El Shaddai. Of the thirty one times this title, God Almighty or the Almighty, is used in Job, thirty times it is used by Job or his friends as they expressed their views and impressions of God. His friends were rebuked (Job 42.7,8). The remaining time it is used, it is used by Jehovah in Job 40.1,2, within the section of the book in which Jehovah responds to Job using His power, as seen in creation, to impress Job with his nothingness, and to give to Job a more accurate understanding of what omnipotence means. (Job 38.1 - 41.34). "Where were you when I laid the foundation of the earth? Declare to Me, if you have and know understanding." (Job 38.4 AMP). God continues to describe how He has limited the oceans and clothed them (vv.8-11), "commanded the morning ... caused the dawn to know its place, ... explored the springs of the sea ... walked in the recesses of the deep." (Job 38.12-18 AMP). God asks if Job knows "By what way is the light distributed, ... who hath prepared gullies in the sky for the torrents of rain or a path for the thunderbolt?" (Job 38.24-30 AMP). Following this He asks whether Job knew the "ordinances of the heavens" and "their rule upon the earth" (vv.31-33 AMP) and whether he had controlled the clouds, rain and lightenings (vv.34-38) before asking Job to consider animal and bird characteristics, habits and abilities (Job 38.39 - 41.34). He intersperses such with references to His might in relation to mankind, referring to the strength of His arm and voice, His honour and majesty as He rules the world, the venting of His anger, His ability to humiliate the proud with a glance, and to tread down the wicked, "bury them in the dust" and "imprison in the house of death." (Job 40.9-14 AMP).

Such a detailed display of the power of God in the macroscopic and microscopic features of creation caused Job to confess, "I know that Thou canst do all things, and that no thought or purpose of Thine can be restrained or thwarted. "(Thou hast said to me) Who is this that darkens and obscures counsel by words without knowledge? Therefore (I see now) I have rashly uttered what I did not understand, things too wonderful for me, which I did not know." (Job 42.2,3 AMP).

God's omnipotence as seen in creation, remains throughout Scripture a source of wonder and worship. The four living creatures are found in Revelation 4.8 saying, "Holy, holy, holy, Lord God Almighty, which was, and is, and is to come." To which the twenty four elders respond, yielding up their crowns, "Thou are worthy, O Lord, to receive glory and honour and power: for Thou hast created all things, and for Thy pleasure they are and were created." (Rev. 4.11). It behoves us to respond as the Psalmist, "Let all inhabitants of the world stand in awe of Him." (Ps. 33.8). Who indeed is able even to count the monuments of His power?

The heavens and the earth once created needed control, preservation and perpetuation which in itself is a study into the omnipotence of God. As to lowly things we read in Job 8.11, "Can the rush grow up without mire? can the flag (reeds) grow without water?" - He provides. As to man and beast Psalm 36.6 asserts, "O Lord, Thou preservest man and beast." As for the seas we hear God declare "Hitherto shalt thou come, but no further: and here shall thy proud waves be stayed." (Job 38.11). Indeed the writer to the Hebrews states, He upholdeth "all things by the word of His power." (Heb. 1.3).

In the context of the majesty of God, among other breathtaking events, we read in Habakkuk 3.6 of His power to scatter mountains and cause hills to bow and then, "and there was the hiding of His power." (3.4) i.e. these things hide more than they reveal of His power - as the ocean hides far more of the iceberg than it permits to be revealed. Again in Job 26.7-13, His might is such that, "He stretcheth out the north ... and hangeth the earth upon nothing ... By His spirit He hath garnished the heavens." Then we read, "Lo, these are parts of His ways" (v.14). We must be found asking, 'And what is the full extent of His power and of His ways!!' Yet, when this creation has served His purposes, then it will be His to fold them up as a vesture (see Heb. 1.12).

The contemplations of the hymn-writer are well expressed

'O Lord my God! When I in awesome wonder
Consider all the works Thy hands have made:
I see the stars, I hear the mighty thunder,
Thy pow'r throughout the universe displayed:
Then sings my soul, my Saviour God to Thee
How great Thou art! How great Thou art!'

THE NATIONS

The origin and distribution of nations is traceable in the book of Genesis. In chapter 9.18-19 we learn, "The sons of Noah, that went forth of the ark, were Shem, and Ham, and Japheth ... and of them was the whole earth overspread." In chapter 10.2-5 twelve families come from Japheth, in verses 6-20 twenty six families come from Ham and in verses 21-31 twenty families stem from Shem. Of each family we read in verses 5,20,31, "After their families, after their tongues, in their lands and in their nations." This was by no means haphazard as Deuteronomy 32.8 asserts, "The Most High divided to the nations their inheritance, when He separated the sons of Adam, He set the bounds of the people ... ." This God claims in Isaiah 44.7, "I appointed the ancient people." Thus Paul preaching in Athens declares, "God that made the world and all things therein ... (Acts 17.24), hath made of one blood all nations of men for to dwell on all the face of the earth, and hath determined the times before appointed, and the bounds of their habitation." (v.26). Hence of His hand we find the nations of Japheth in the north, those of Ham in the south, and those of Shem in the central belt.

But in addition to bounds, Acts 17.26 states that times are by His appointment i.e. the times of the rise and fall of kings and empires. Remarkably this verse maintains that the times were preappointed by God i.e. before the nations existed. Thus Jeremiah shows that Judah's looking to Egypt for help against Nebuchadnezzar was futile, since "Pharaoh king of Egypt is but a noise; for he hath passed the time appointed." (Jer. 46.17).

Similarly when Israel left Egypt in the days of Moses and entered Canaan - God meted out judgment to both Egypt and Canaan in keeping with Genesis 15.13-16, where Egypt's relation with Israel is described, "They shall afflict them four hundred years; and also that nation, whom they shall serve, will I judge: and afterward shall they come out. ... In the fourth generation they shall come hither (Canaan) again: for the iniquity of the Amorites is not yet full."

That same power among the nations is evident in Daniel 4.17, "The Most High ruleth in the kingdom of men, and giveth it to whomsoever He will."

This is most reassuring, since the government of nations is far more than appears. Human rulers rule according to Romans 13, but behind them are unseen powers. Daniel 10.13,20,21, illustrate something of the struggles behind the scenes, and Ezekiel 28 shows the power behind the power - as indeed does Revelation 12 show that the power behind the beast of Revelation 13 is the dragon, (compare ch.12.9 and ch.13.4).

In Isaiah 24.21 we are shown that, "In that day, (the Day of the Lord) ... the Lord shall punish the host of the high ones that are on high, and the kings of the earth upon the earth." The punishment clearly relates to that in Revelation 19.19-21 where John saw the beast and the kings of the earth and their armies gathered together to make war against Him. Of the beast and the false prophet we read, "both were cast alive into a lake of fire burning with brimstone." (Rev. 19.20).

As has become evident, not only do men and the powers of darkness influence the government of nations, but so also does God and His holy angels. This is the result of His possessing absolute, all-embracing power - He is not just mighty but almighty, omnipotent.

This omnipotence among nations has been manifested in the overrule of the duration of governments at an international level, particularly during the "Times of the Gentiles" (Lk. 21.24) - a period of Gentile supremacy commencing with the rise of Nebuchadnezzar and terminating with the dawn of the millennial reign of Christ. Examples of God's omnipotence during this period are many and one or two will suffice. In Daniel 5.26-28, of Belshazzar it is written, that he had been "weighed in the balances, and found wanting". Thus his kingdom had been "numbered and brought to an end," by his rule passing to the Medes and Persians. At the instigation of a higher court than sits on earth, the great Gentile monarch was deposed, and Darius who reigned contemporaneously with Cyrus (see Isaiah 45) received the kingdom.

Similarly Isaiah chapters 13-23, demonstrate God's power among at least ten nations, both with regard to immediate and far distant issues. A power which can begin to be appreciated as we understand that "The nations are as a drop of a bucket, and are counted as the small dust of the balance: ... All nations before Him are as nothing; and they are counted to Him less than nothing, and vanity." (Is. 40.15,17). Most remarkable, however, is the exercise of that unique power to achieve His ends, whilst men think they are achieving theirs, without any overseeing influences, let alone God.

Jeremiah who had a prophetic role similar to that of Isaiah is referred to in Jeremiah 1.10 as being by the Lord, "set ... over the nations and over the kingdoms, to root out, and to pull down, and to destroy, and to throw down, to build, and to plant." Such a ministry will be superseded by Christ who not only foretells but will be responsible for the conclusion of the times of the Gentiles (Dan. 2.44) and the ensuing judgment of the living nations (Mt. 25.31-46) at the Throne of His Glory.

THE JEW

When asked by Frederick the Great for an unanswerable proof, in one word, of the inspiration of the Bible, the court preacher replied - 'The Jew'. Appropriately, the emblem of the race is a bush burning but not being consumed. For thousands of years, amid all civilisations and countries there has continued to exist a distinct people with laws, habits and customs distinctly their own. Though oppressed and scattered among the nations, they have reappeared on the page of modern history and will proceed to become the head and not the tail of the nations - see Deuteronomy 28.13. - so is the word of omnipotence.

Sovereignly chosen from among the nations, divinely loved for no other reason than that the Lord loved them - for they were but a small people and not attractive, in faithfulness to His oath and promise to the patriarchs, the Lord brought them out of bondage and from the hand of Pharaoh with a mighty hand (Deut. 7.6-8). Says verse 9 "know therefore that the Lord thy God, He is God, the faithful God, which keepeth covenant and mercy with them that love Him and keep his commandments to a thousand generations" - what attributes! what power is implicated!

In Isaiah 45.4, despite His people's many wayward experiences, God tells Cyrus, "For Jacob My servant's sake, and Israel Mine elect, I have even called thee by thy name: I have surnamed thee, though thou hast not known Me." - remarkable indeed! We will not be surprised that in Isaiah 40.18 He challenges human thought by asking, "To whom then will ye liken God?" and proceeds by asserting, "It is He that sitteth upon the circle (sphere) of the earth, ... That bringeth the princes to nothing." (vv.22,23). And then again in verse 25 He repeats His challenge, "To whom then will ye liken Me, or shall I be equal? saith the Holy One." No human voice responds, so He appeals to the witness of creation in verse 26. How small is man's appreciation of these things and of the God whose power is exhibited!

It is such an One that in verse 27 can turn to His people and enquire, "Why sayest thou, O Jacob, and speakest, O Israel, My way is hid from the Lord, and my judgment is passed over from my God?" And then asks, "Hast thou not known? hast thou not heard, that the everlasting God, the Lord, the Creator of the ends of the earth, fainteth not, neither is weary? there is no searching of His understanding. He giveth power to the faint; and to them that have no might He increaseth strength." (vv.28-29).

Despite His love (Deut. 7.7-8), His choice (Is. 45.4 and Rom. 11.28), His covenant (Gen. 15), His gifts and His use of His people of which Paul writes in Romans 9.4,5, "To whom pertaineth the adoption, and the glory, and the covenants, and the giving of the law, and the service of God, and the promises; whose are the fathers, and of whom as concerning the flesh Christ came." Again in chapter 3.2, "Unto them were committed the oracles of God," - despite all these things, captivity and dispersion were the only possible reactions of God in righteousness to their unrighteousness, and to their cry of Matthew 27.25, "His blood be on us, and on our children."

Yet Paul could ask, knowing that only a negative answer would be appropriate, "Hath God cast away His people?" (Rom. 11.1) and then in verse 2 reassuringly asserts, "God hath not cast away His people which He foreknew." Indeed at present, "There is a remnant according to the election of grace." (v.5), and of the future, (v.23), "God is able to graff them in again." For verse 25, "blindness in part is happened to Israel, until the fulness of the Gentiles be come in."

All this is in keeping with Hosea 3.4,5, "The children of Israel shall abide many days without a king, and without a prince, and without a sacrifice, and without an image, and without an ephod, and without teraphim. Afterward shall the children of Israel return ... and shall fear the Lord." And as prophesied by Christ Himself in Luke 21.24, "They shall fall by the edge of the sword, and shall be led away captive into all nations: and Jerusalem shall be trodden down of the Gentiles, until the times of the Gentiles be fulfilled." - so confirming Daniel 2.44. Conviction of such enabled James, at the Jerusalem conference, (Acts. 15.6-29) to say, "Known unto God are all His works from the beginning of the world." (v.18).

Hence at the sound of the trumpet of Matthew 24.31, God's power toward His earthly people will be evident in a variety of ways:-

(a) His power of discrimination - Jeremiah 30.10,11, "Fear thou not, ... I will save thee from afar, and thy seed from the land of their captivity; ... though I make a full end of all nations whither I have scattered thee, yet will I not make a full end of thee: but I will correct thee in measure."

(b) His power of restoration - Amos 9.14-15, "They shall build the waste cities ... I will plant them upon their land, and they shall no more be pulled up out of their land." - Hosea 2.19, "I will betroth thee unto me for ever."

(c) His power of repetition - Isaiah 11.11, "In that day ... the Lord shall set His hand again a second time to recover the remnant of His people." - Jeremiah 16.14,15, "Behold the days come, saith the Lord, that it shall no more be said, The Lord liveth, that brought up the children of Israel out of the land of Egypt; But, The Lord liveth, that brought up the children of Israel from the land of the north, and from all the lands whither He had driven them."

(d) His power to pledge - Jeremiah 31.35,36, "Thus saith the Lord, which giveth the sun for a light by day, and the ordinances of the moon and of the stars for a light by night, which divideth the sea when the waves thereof roar; The Lord of hosts is His name: If those ordinances depart from before Me, saith the Lord, then the seed of Israel also shall cease from being a nation before Me for ever."

(e) His power of preservation - Zechariah 13.8,9 "In all the land, saith the Lord, two parts therein shall be cut off and die; but the third shall be left therein. And I will bring the third part through the fire, and will refine them ... I will say, It is My people."

(f) His power of national resurrection - Ezekiel 37.11, "Our bones are dried, and our hope is lost: we are cut off for our parts." To which the Lord God responds, "Behold, O My people, I will open your graves, and cause you to come up out of your graves, and bring you into the land of Israel. ... then shall ye know that I the Lord have spoken it, and performed it." (vv.12-14).

(g) His power to reunite - Ezekiel 37.22 "I will make them one nation in the land ... and one king shall be king to them all: and they shall be no more two nations, neither shall they be divided into two kingdoms any more at all."

(h) His power in conversion - Ezekiel 36.24, "I ... will bring you into your own land. Then (v.25) will I ... cleanse you. A new heart also will I give you, and a new spirit will I put within you (v.26). Ye shall be My people, and I will be your God (v.28)."

(i) His power of timing - Daniel 9.24, "Seventy weeks are determined upon thy people and upon thy holy city, to ... make an end of sins ... bring in everlasting righteousness ... and to anoint the most Holy."

Little wonder that Isaiah could write, "All flesh shall know that I the Lord am thy Saviour and thy Redeemer, the mighty One of Jacob." (Is. 49.26).

THE CHURCH

This people, crossing the boundary of Jew and Gentile, (Eph. 2.14-16), the latter the more surprising entity (Acts 15.14), was introduced by the Lord Himself as being invincible. For said He, "The gates of hell shall not prevail against it." (Mt. 16.18). It is the express project of our Lord, "I will build My church." The characteristics of those who comprise the edifice are geared to enhance in our minds His power and so direct all glory to God (1 Cor. 1.26-31). For despite the poverty of such, in as much as they are in Christ (v.30), they possess that which influence, education, money, status and power cannot achieve or purchase. Further, by Him they are fully equipped to effect His purposes in this present scene (1 Cor. 1.5-7).

The building process is dependent on that which to the Jew is a stumbling block and to the Gentiles, foolishness i.e. "Christ crucified" - the apparent essence of weakness and absence of wisdom. Yet Christ is the Exponent of God's wisdom and power (1 Cor. 1.24), and the desired ends will be achieved, not in spite of but in light of His crucifixion.

The preaching of Christ crucified, i.e. the Gospel, is the declared, "power of God unto salvation." (Rom 1.16) - the word power being the translation of the word dunamis from which we get our word dynamite. This power, being exerted presently to spiritual ends, is not understood as to its might and effect. Hence Paul prays, "The eyes of your understanding being enlightened; that ye may know ... what is the exceeding greatness of His power to us-ward who believe." (Eph. 1.18-23) - to effect chapter 2.1, the quickening of those "dead in trespasses and sins." That power, Paul says, is that which was involved in the quickening, ascension and exaltation of Christ, and these were, "according to the working of His mighty power" (1.19). Similarly the members of the church have been "quickened" (2.5), "raised" (2.6) and "made sit together in heavenly places", in virtue of the same power.

The power of God not only brings us into this new life and sphere of living, but into a new relationship. "And will be a Father unto you, and ye shall be My sons and daughters, saith the Lord Almighty." (2 Cor. 6.18), and provides the enabling for such a life, inasmuch as we are indwelt by the Spirit of God.

God, being omnipotent, "is able to do exceeding abundantly" - i.e. beyond all means of computation, "above all that we ask or think." In keeping with His mind and purposes and according to the power that worketh in us, He is able to strengthen with might by His Spirit, stimulate affection for Christ, enable us to grasp with all saints the length, breadth, depth and height (of the mystery or His love?), know the unknowable i.e. the love of Christ which passes knowledge, and be filled with all the fulness of God. (Eph. 3.16-20).

We can share Paul's confidence in these matters, "He is able to keep that which I have committed unto Him against that day." (2 Tim. 1.12). Further we "are kept by the power of God through faith unto salvation ready to be revealed in the last time." (1 Pet. 1.5). Presently, conscious of our weakness, we can draw strength from 2 Corinthians 13.4, "He was crucified through weakness, yet He liveth by the power of God. For we also are weak in Him, but we shall live with Him by the power of God toward you." Even as Peter declares, "Divine power hath given unto us all things that pertain unto life and godliness." (2 Pet. 1.3) and Paul confirms in Colossians 1.11 where we read we are, "strengthened with all might" and empowered with all power (if all, then limitless) - "according to His glorious power, unto all patience, and long suffering with joyfulness." This entails development which Paul recognised in Acts 20.32 when he commended the Ephesians, "to God, and to the word of His grace, which is able to build you up," while they waited for the giving of the inheritance. An inheritance which is, "Incorruptible, and undefiled, and that fadeth not away, reserved in heaven for you, who are (yourselves) kept by the power of God." (1 Pet. 1.4-5).

While we wait for such, we are expected to witness. For this occupation, 2 Corinthians 4.7 reminds us, "We have this treasure in earthen vessels that the excellency of the power may be of God, and not of us." In fact all service is in dependence of His power and authority. "To Him we stand or fall." With the Bema in view, Romans 14.4 assures us, "God is able to make him stand." Again, in the context of giving for the needy, "He is able to make all grace abound." (2 Cor. 9.8). Hence a cheerful giver, thanks to His grace, is enabled to continue giving, since He ensures sufficiency.

If we fear ourselves, and failure and shortcoming concern us, then we can encourage ourselves that, He "is able," (Jude 24) "to keep you from falling, and to present you faultless before the presence of His glory with exceeding joy."

With such assurances we will no doubt continue with Jude and say, "To the only wise God our Saviour be glory and majesty, dominion and power, both now and ever. Amen." (v.25).

CHRIST

Being what His name Emmanuel implies - God with us, (Mt. 1.23) then of Him we can read in John 1.1 that He was in the beginning, He was with God and that He was God. Hence all the attributes essential to Deity have, are, and ever will be His. He is the sole Creator. (Jn. 1.3). All these essentials are confirmed of the Son of His love in Colossians 1.15-17. A passage which asserts that He is not only the firstborn of all creation but also firstborn from the dead. Hence "in all things", including the new creation of 2 Corinthians 5.17, "He might have the preeminence."

Born into this scene to Mary who had been told that the Holy Ghost would come upon her, and the power of the Highest overshadow her (Lk. 1.35), He continued to be what He always was, as Colossians 2.9 states, "In Him dwelleth all the fulness of the Godhead bodily" i.e. He whom the heaven and heaven of heavens cannot contain (1 Kings 8.27) was found in totality in a body prepared by God (Heb. 10.5). His life was summarised by Peter in Acts 2.22 "Jesus of Nazareth, a man approved of God among you by miracles and wonders and signs, which God did by Him in the midst of you." He allayed John Baptist's fears regarding His identity by the reply of Luke 7.22, "Tell John what things ye have seen and heard; how that the blind see, the lame walk, the lepers are cleansed, the deaf hear, the dead are raised, to the poor the gospel is preached." Not only did our Lord display such amazing power, but He had the ability as in Luke 9.1 to call "His twelve disciples together, and gave them power over all devils, and to cure diseases." When in Mark 9.23 (RV) His disciples said, "If Thou canst" it was with a sharp rebuke that He replied, "All things are possible to Him that believeth."

Men, even disciples, may query His identity and ability, but on a high mountain (Mt. 17.1-6) the Father unequivocally declared, out of the cloud, "This is My beloved Son, in whom I am well pleased; hear ye Him." - enabling Peter to claim, "We have not followed cunningly devised fables, when we made known unto you the power and coming of our Lord Jesus Christ, but were eyewitnesses of His majesty." (2 Pet.

1.16).

As to His life, which was miraculous as to conception, He said in John 10.18 "No man taken it from Me ... I have power to lay it down and I have power to take it again." And when challenged by Pilate with the words, "Knowest Thou not that I have power to crucify Thee and have power to release Thee?" He could reply, "Thou couldest have no power against Me except it were given thee from above." (Jn. 19.10,11). He had to first be "delivered by the determinate counsel and foreknowledge of God" before it could be said, "Ye have taken and by wicked hands have crucified and slain." (Acts 2.23). Even in the process of trying to take Him in the garden "they went backward, and fell to the ground," in reaction to His reply "I am." (Jn. 18.4-6).

But why, it may be asked, when possessing inherently such absolute power, did He yield to them? Hebrews 2.14,15 supplies the answer, because it was "Through death He might destroy him that had the power of death, that is, the devil; and deliver them who through fear of death were all their lifetime subject to bondage." Again in Colossians 2.15 we read, "Having spoiled principalities and powers, He made a show of them openly, triumphing over them in it."

Such a display would require that He did take His life again (Jn. 10.18) enabling Paul to write, "To this end Christ both died, and rose, and revived, that He might be Lord both of the dead and living." (Rom. 14.9), and thus qualifying Christ to preface the commission of Matthew 28.18, "All power is given unto Me in heaven and in earth" i.e. omnipotence is Mine. The taking again of His life meant in the words of Romans 1.4 that He was "Declared ... Son of God with power, according to the spirit of holiness, by the resurrection from the dead." Here is the power to which Paul appealed in Ephesians 1.19-22, "which He wrought in Christ, when He raised Him from (among) the dead, and set Him at His own right hand in the heavenly places, far above ... all things under His feet." Here is the position to which Peter refers, "Who is gone into heaven, and is on the right hand of God; angels and authorities and powers being made subject unto Him." (1 Pet. 3.22).

In such exaltation He has been called of God to be High Priest, "Not after the law of a carnal commandment, but after the power of an endless life." (Heb. 7.16). The same One declares Himself to be, "Alpha and Omega, the beginning and the ending, saith the Lord, which is, and which was, and which is to come, the Almighty." (Rev. 1.8), and in verse 18 has "the keys of hell and of death." In chapter 2.26 He is able to promise to delegate to the overcomer, "power over the nations", whilst He Himself is declared worthy to receive, among other things, unspecified power. The reason given in chapter 4.11 is "Thou hast created all things, and for Thy pleasure they are and were created," and in chapter 5.12 it is because He was slain. Anticipating that which is still future, John heard heaven and earth saying, "Blessing, and honour, and glory, and power, be unto Him that sitteth upon the throne, and unto the Lamb for ever and ever." (Rev. 5.13).

Sadly, such anticipation is not shared by all, hence the need to remove all forms of opposition. For such, the Day of the Lord will come, "as a destruction from the Almighty." (Joel 1.15). Satan is to be "cast out into the earth, and his angels", to the accompaniment of a loud voice in heaven saying, "Now is come salvation, and strength, and the kingdom of our God, and the power of His Christ: for the accuser of our brethren is cast down." (Rev. 12.9-10). For saints on earth, the tribulation will be intensified and many will seal their testimony with their blood. Yet Revelation 15.2,3 assure us that it is they that have "gotten the victory" and are found singing, "Great and marvellous are Thy works, Lord God Almighty." Thus when the great whore mystery Babylon the great has been judged (Rev.17), and the great city Babylon has known its judgment (Rev.18), then as Revelation 19.5-6 prophesies, all His servants will respond to the voice from the throne with an ever increasing crescendo of voices saying, "Alleluia: for the Lord God omnipotent reigneth." A fact that all on earth soon appreciate, for "Heaven opened, and behold a white horse; and He that sat upon him was called Faithful and True, and in righteousness He doth judge and make war." (Rev. 19.11). The name written on His thigh, "KING OF KINGS AND LORD OF

LORDS" (v.16) soon becomes a fact of life, as Isaiah 45.23 and Philippians 2.10-11 are realised and "every knee bows", and "every tongue confesses, that Jesus Christ is Lord, to the glory of God the Father." With Satan bound, and Christ's powerful rule established in accord with Psalm 2.9, the millennium reign can be enjoyed. But Satan must be finally removed (Rev. 20.10). And because John 5.27 declares the Son has authority, "to execute judgment also", then, no doubt at His command, John records "The sea gave up the dead which were in it; and death and hell delivered up the dead which were in them: and they were judged every man according to their works." (Rev. 20.13). But 1 Corinthians 15.25 declares, "He must reign, till He hath put all enemies under His feet." Then as Revelation 20.14 is enacted, the sense of finality is to be enjoyed for we read, "The last enemy that shall be destroyed is death." (1 Cor. 15.26).

At this point, His reign in the presence of enemies will terminate. For it is as the One who puts "down all rule and all authority and power" that He reigns. (1 Cor. 15.24). When His omnipotence is acknowledged by all creation of whatever order, rank or realm, "then cometh the end."

He who cried, "It is finished: and He bowed His head, and gave up the ghost (Jn. 19.30), will, with the satisfaction of having completed the work of the ages, deliver "up the kingdom to God, even the Father." (1 Cor. 15.24) - who as the Throne Sitter of Revelation 21.5, in the eternal state, declares, "Behold, I make all things new." To such an announcement the One who is confessedly, "Alpha and Omega, the beginning and the end" replies as ever, "IT IS DONE" (v.6).

What omnipotence!

Thus in relation to creation, the Gentiles, the Jew and the church His power is seen to be almighty power. He can carry all the responsibilities and meet all the demands upon His power not in sequence but simultaneously. Again we, in light of His omnipotence, exclaim, 'How great Thou art!'

The Essential Attributes of God

THE ETERNITY OF GOD

By Ian Jackson

The salient doctrine of the Bible is that which concerns God Himself. It is true that in creation there is revealed "His eternal power and Godhead" (Rom. 1.20) but God has given us His Word that in its pages we might come to know Him personally. Indeed, it may be confidently affirmed that the whole of the Bible is the revelation of God, His nature, character, purposes and ways and all that we can know of God personally is revealed in Scripture. It may be further affirmed that such knowledge can only be obtained there. The person who seeks to know God will do so through the reading and study of the Word, by meditating upon it and obeying it. This should, of course, be the consuming desire of every Christian as it was of Paul who counted all things but loss for His knowledge (Phil. 3.8).

It follows that we can only know God by faith. Faith is the ready, confident acceptance of what God has said. The only person who knows God and can increase in His knowledge is the man or woman of faith. In ancient times Zophar, one of Job's friends, asked, "Canst thou by searching find out God?" (Job 11.7). God is not discoverable by human enquiry and rational, logical deduction. To know God it is necessary for faith to apprehend that which God has revealed.

Although the present world shrinks from dogmatic assertions as to the nature, character and attributes of God, His revelation of Himself is true to the exclusion of all other ideas of God that men possess. There are those who are called 'gods' in heaven and in earth but the true and living God alone has revealed Himself. "There is none other God but one" (1 Cor. 8.4). "To us there is but one God" (1 Cor. 8.6). He is not the creation of imagination, superstition or self-awareness, nor does He reside in nature but He is the almighty, transcendent, glorious Lord. Man-made gods have the characteristics imagined by man; the God of the Bible has inherent attributes which are eternal and immutable. These have not been conferred upon Him: He is eternally "the Same". He has revealed Himself in His Word.

There is no greater knowledge than the knowledge of God. Whilst large sums of money are invested annually to secure an increase in the knowledge of earthly, material things the Christian has a capacity, by the Holy Spirit, freely to ascend heights not accessible in any other field of enquiry and knowledge. With a humble mind, a contrite heart, a prayerful attitude and an open Bible the Christian can know his God. This privilege is also the chief responsibility of a Christian. That there is an ever present need for appropriating by faith what God has revealed of Himself in His Word is evident from the fact that true spiritual maturity is measured by whether or not we know Him (1 Jn. 2.13,14).

In approaching this, however, there has to be a recognition that there is that about God which is unknowable save by God Himself. His ways are higher than ours; His thoughts likewise (Is. 55.9). Recognition of this fact will ensure that conjecture is eliminated from our thinking and that revelation will not be brought to the bar of human reason. Frail humanity stands in puzzled bewilderment at the interface of time and eternity. Bound by limitations of time and space we find it impossible properly to conceive the infinitude of eternity and the High and Lofty One who inhabits it (Is. 57.15). As a child might stand ankle-deep at the ocean's edge so we stand in the shallows of the unbounded sea of the divine Being.

Yet, for all this, doctrine is generally undervalued in the present day. It is a sad fact that it is out of vogue. For many, a diet of doctrine seems to lead to spiritual indigestion. Devotional and practical encouragements, exhortations, illustrations and anecdotes are usually considered to be more palatable. Doctrine, it is said, tends to legalism; the practice of Christianity is far more important. Such is the shallow thinking which pervades the beginning of the third millennium A.D. Perhaps the spirit of the age, in which there are no absolutes (for everything has sunk into the morass of relativism) has affected Christians.

We are truly unable to comprehend eternity. It is hard enough to comprehend time. One long ago said, 'If no man will ask me the question, what time is, I know well enough what it is; but if any will ask me what it is, I know not how to explain it.' We may speak of eternity in similar fashion. Knowing only a succession, minutes, hours, days, months, seasons and years we more easily understand the fact of eternity than its nature. Even the writers of the inspired Word find themselves limited to using words which relate to time to express the eternal.

Certain things are spoken of in Scripture as being perpetual, eternal or everlasting which are truly of long duration but will, in fact, have an end. For instance, the Hebrew slave who decided to forego his liberty in the seventh year on account of his love for his master, would be marked by the aul thrust through his ear and he would be his servant "for ever" (Deut. 15.17). This clearly does not extend into eternity but marks the long duration of his service here. Similarly, when speaking of angels and the souls of men, the Bible speaks in terms of that which is everlasting or eternal yet these, though they have no end, had a beginning and are not therefore eternal as God is eternal.

God, however, is without beginning or end. Moses, possessed of the knowledge of the frailty of man, exclaims that "from everlasting to everlasting Thou art God" (Ps. 90.2). The first and fourth books of Psalms (Psalms 41 and 106) end with ascriptions of praise to the Lord God of Israel "from everlasting to everlasting". The eternal God (Deut. 33.27) and the everlasting God (Is. 40.28; Rom. 16.26) whose name is from everlasting (Is. 63.16) stands, as such, unique in His universe. He is unoriginated; He will never cease to be.

Time carries with it the idea that something precedes it. When we think of eternity there is nothing before it; if there were it would not then be eternity. Time also suggests that there is that which will succeed it: the very nature of time is that it consists in succession. Time is a measure of change. In contrast eternity is an infinite and unchanging duration, a fixed and permanent state.

That God is eternal is, in a sense, axiomatic. God would not be God if He were not supreme: He could not be supreme if His coming into existence depended upon another or even if it depended upon Himself, for that would mean that He was once without existence and therefore nothing. In the same manner God could not be God if there was that which could bring about the cessation of His existence or even if He Himself brought it about.

The Christian then can find great consolations in the fact that God is "the Same" (Ps. 102.27; Heb. 1.12; 13.8). This is, indeed, one of the names of God expressing His immutability, the One upon whom we can rely in the changing circumstances of life. Eternity means immutability. Eternity negates any thought of succession: the eternal God is "the Same".

Not only is God eternal but He is uniquely so. This is an attribute of God which is incommunicable: it belongs alone to Him. Accordingly, although man from the first has harboured desires to be like God (Gen. 3.5) and in a coming day one will sit in the temple of God portraying himself as God (2 Thess. 2.4), God alone is possessed of eternity of being and such ambition is therefore bound to fail. He stands apart from all that he has brought into existence for all the creation exists by His power. God is creation's cause but He had no prior cause. He is the effect of nothing. God stands alone in the glory of His eternity.

John reminds us that "All things were made by Him, and without Him was not anything made that was made" (Jn. 1.3). In so saying John makes it abundantly clear that He is excluded from the totality of created things. Anything that has been made had its origin in God and He is Himself without origin.

At the burning bush God is able to identify Himself to Moses as "I AM THAT I AM" (Ex. 3.14). Newberry, in 'The Englishman's Bible', points out that literally the expression is, 'I will be that I will be' but that as the so-called future or long tense expresses not simply the future but also, and especially, continuance, the force is 'I continue to be, and will be, what I continue to be, and will be'. It has been said that God knows no past, no present, and no future but only one eternal now.

In this connection it should be noted that 'Jehovah' has the significance of 'He that always was, that always is, and that ever is to come'. He is unconditioned by time.

Before the hills in order stood,
Or earth received her frame,
From everlasting Thou art God,
To endless years the Same.'

The eternity of the separate persons in the Godhead is undeniably established in Scripture. Denial of the deity of the Lord Jesus and the Holy Spirit is thus seen to be heterodox. That the Father is eternal, is, apparently, universally accepted by those who claim to base their beliefs on the Bible. That the Son and Holy Spirit are also eternal, as being divine, is universally accepted by those who are saved.

Insofar as the Holy Spirit of God is concerned Scripture abounds in proofs of His personality and speaks of Him as "the eternal Spirit" (Heb. 9.14). This ends all debate as to whether the Holy Spirit is divine; only God is eternal. The same is true of the Lord Jesus, "whose goings forth have been from of old, from everlasting" (Mic. 5.2). The significance of 'everlasting' in this verse is 'from the days of eternity'. This much mistranslated Scripture (various translations speak of His 'origins' despite the fact that the verse is actually teaching that He is without origin) would by itself demonstrate the eternity and divinity of the Lord Jesus, yet there are numerous others. John, in his gospel, does not speak with the other evangelists of the birth of the Lord Jesus as such; rather, he speaks of the incarnation of the Word. The Word, who was made flesh and dwelt among us, is the eternal Word. The profoundly simple opening of this gospel indicates the unoriginated, pre-beginning existence of the Word who was not only with God but was God. We may anticipate such statements at the beginning of this gospel, avowedly written "that ye might believe that Jesus is the Christ, the Son of God" (Jn 20.31). In his first epistle, written to establish the true humanity of the Lord Jesus, John makes the same point in speaking of "that eternal life which was with the Father" (1 Jn.1.2). The force of the statement is that there was never a time when the Lord Jesus, the personification of eternal life, was not with the Father. He was with Him to all eternity.

It is most instructive to note the use of the word 'before' in connection with the Lord Jesus.

John 1.15,30 John the Baptist said of Him, "He was before me". It is well known that, in fact, John's birth pre-dated the birth of the Lord Jesus by some six months and the confession that John makes can therefore only be understood in terms of his referring to His pre-existence.

John 17.5 The Lord Jesus, in prayer to the Father, refers to the glory which He had with Him "before the world was". To all eternity He shared with the Father all the glory of deity.

John 17.24 Again, in prayer, the Lord Jesus refers to the fact of the Father's love which he had known "before the foundation of the world".

Colossians 1.16,17 Paul, in speaking of creation coming into existence in, by and for the Lord Jesus says that "He is before all things".

John 8.58 Here the Lord Jesus gives one of the clearest attestations of Scripture to His deity and eternity. He has told His sceptical audience that their father Abraham had rejoiced to see His day. Incredulous, the people reminded Him that He was not yet fifty years old: how could He have seen Abraham? Our Saviour replied, "Before Abraham was I am". It has often been noted that he did not say, "Before Abraham was I was", for that would be true of angels, demons and the devil. Here is a statement of eternity and deity, our Lord thereby identifying Himself as the God of the burning bush who announced Himself to be the "I AM". Truly the mystery of godliness is great (1 Tim. 3.16). Here is One who is truly man, moving within a sphere of time and space, making irrefutable statements as to His eternity, deity and infinity. Before such a person redeemed hearts can only bow in wonder and adoration.

The Lord Jesus, the Alpha and Omega, is the One "which is and, which was, and which is to come" (Rev. 1.8), a title which corresponds to the Hebrew name of Jehovah. He is the One who always is, who ever was and who is always the coming One. Truly He is "the first and the last" (Rev. 1.17). With gladness the heart of the believer hears the Father addressing the Son, saying, "Thou art the Same" (Heb. 1.12). Well may we sing:-

'Thou art the everlasting Word,
The Father's only Son;
God manifestly seen and heard,
And heaven's beloved One:
Worthy, O Lamb of God art Thou,
That every knee to Thee should bow.'

The relationship of the persons in the Godhead is also eternal and, therefore, immutable. It has already been noted that the Holy Spirit is eternal; it is not just that He had no beginning of subsistence but also He is eternally the Spirit. He did not become the Holy Spirit at any particular time such as when He was sent forth (Gal. 4.6); the One who was sent was the Spirit. His being sent forth manifested His true character as the Spirit of God. There was never a moment when the relationship between the Father and the Holy Spirit either began or, as to its nature, changed. Equally, there was never a time when the Lord Jesus became the Son of God. He is that to all eternity.

The denial of the eternal sonship of the Lord Jesus is a most serious matter. Though there are areas of doctrine where believers may differ in conviction yet happily enjoy fellowship together, it must always be remembered that error in respect of the person and work of Christ is costly. The Lord Jesus Himself said, for instance, that a denial of His deity would ensure that the person so denying would die in his sins (Jn. 8.24). One cannot deny His deity and be saved. The denial of the eternal sonship is surely the first step in the slippery slope of heterodox teaching regarding Christ's person which has stained the history of christian testimony, not least in the last two hundred years.

That glorious truth has been denied by both commentators and translators. The assertions made by some that the Lord Jesus became the Son of God at birth; or only realised He was the Son at His baptism, when heaven was opened and His sonship affirmed; or was at some time adopted by God as His Son, are without any biblical foundation. He did not become the Son at His incarnation: it was at that time that God sent forth His Son (Gal. 4.4). He must have been the Son of God before being sent forth or God could not have sent forth 'His Son'. To this the Scriptures bear unequivocal testimony.

John tells us that "the only begotten Son" (an expression bearing testimony to unoriginated relationship and special affection) "which is in the bosom of the Father, He hath declared Him" (Jn. 1.18). The grammatical construction is such that the One who is in the bosom of the Father, God's only begotten Son, is indicated as having been there continually in the past, being so in the present and continuously being so in the future. The Father's bosom is not, of course, to be understood as a geographical location but is expressive of the place of mutual affection and love. The thought that He who was in the bosom of the Father was subsequently found in the arms of Mary, signifying the greatness of His condescending stoop to earth, is frequently expressed but it is not really true in that He never left the Father's bosom. He is there eternally as the Son.

The Father expresses the truth of that eternal relationship as on several occasions Scripture records Him saying, "Thou art My Son". Psalm 2.7, where this first occurs, is an important verse regarding Christ's eternal sonship. The Father says here, "Thou art my Son; this day have I begotten Thee". The Father was not saying, 'You are My Son; today I have become Your Father' as this verse is rendered in the NIV; this is at once a denial of the eternal Fatherhood of God and the eternal sonship of the Lord Jesus. Here the Father expresses a timeless and eternal truth; the Lord Jesus is His Son. He affirms at His incarnation that that relationship is unchanged by His incarnation. The term 'begotten' does not connote any idea of generation, as if the Son is junior to, or inferior to, the Father. Rather, it is expressive of relationship.

Before Psalm 2.7 is quoted in Hebrews 1 the writer alludes to Christ's eternal sonship. God has spoken in His Son. When God spoke, after all the prophets had brought their word from God, He spoke in His character as Son. This was God Himself speaking in the person of His Son but this is not to be understood as indicating that the Son was distinct from God as were the prophets. Rather, God speaks as Son. Here is an implicit affirmation of His eternal sonship. Further, the writer is quick to note that it was by the Son that creation came into existence. It was not made by one who became Son but by the One who was then the Son, the appointed heir of all things. Clearly, the passage teaches that His sonship was antecedent to both creation and His incarnation.

Again, redeemed hearts bow at the wonder of His glorious Person. The eternal Son of God is found in true humanity. True manhood and eternal sonship were necessary characteristics in the one raised up in the nation, and for the nation, a Saviour (Acts 13.21-33); who is greater than the angels (Heb.1.5); and who is the High Priest of His people (Heb. 5.5). Psalm 2.7 is, of course, quoted in each of these references.

'Eternal Word, eternal Son,
The Father's constant joy;
What Thou hast done, and what Thou art
Shall all our tongues employ:
Our Lord, our Life, we Thee adore,
Worthy art Thou for evermore.'

It has already been noted that "before the world was" the Lord Jesus shared with the Father all the glory of deity (Jn. 17.5) and that "before the foundation of the world" He was the object of the Father's love (Jn. 17.24). In other Scriptures, using terms similar to these, we are given an insight into divine activity which occurred before the world was brought into existence. It is no surprise to learn in that chapter that before the foundation of the world there was divine purpose relative to the Son of God but we might well bow in thanksgiving as we discover that such purpose also included His people. In reminding the Corinthians that he did not preach to them the gospel with enticing words of man's wisdom Paul indicates that that which he spoke was "the wisdom of God in a mystery, even the hidden mystery, which God ordained before the world unto our glory" (1 Cor. 2.1-8). Divine purpose is centred in the Son of God but the child of God rejoices to know that he has been brought within the scope of that purpose, and not in a way that is merely peripheral. Accordingly, "He hath saved us, and called us with an holy calling, not according to our works, but according to His own purpose and grace, which was given us in Christ Jesus before the world began" (2 Tim. 1.9). Eternal life, too, was promised, "before the world began" (Tit. 1.2).

These are matters which should fill the heart of the believer with gladness. Salvation was not some kind of emergency plan brought in after the fall of man as a salvage operation. Rather, redemption was eternally in the heart of God and to this end the Lamb "was verily foreordained before the foundation of the world, but was manifest in these last times for you, who by Him do believe in God" (1 Pet. 1.20-21).

These references are to be distinguished from those which express the idea of that which has happened 'from the foundation of the world', which have particular reference to divine purpose relative to the nation of Israel. When reference is made to that which was 'before' the world it has particular relevance to believers of this church age and the church which is His Body. The unique position of the church in the purposes and ways of God is thus made clear. The "eternal purpose which He purposed in Christ Jesus our Lord" (Eph. 3.11) has in view the exhibition of God's multifaceted wisdom to principalities and powers by the church, God's masterpiece. That Israel as a nation is not the church, or even part of it, is clear from the teaching of Ephesians 3 that the mystery had been hid in God; in other ages it was not made known as it has now been made known by the apostles and prophets by the Spirit. Gentiles were not within the scope of national promises given to Israel. They were "without Christ, being aliens from the commonwealth of Israel, and strangers from the covenants of promise, having no hope, and without God in the world" (Eph. 2.12). In this present dispensation, however, Gentile believers, together with Jewish believers in the Lord Jesus are fellow-heirs, fellow-members and fellow-partakers of His promise in Christ by the gospel.

It is not surprising, therefore, that in the same epistle Paul notes that believers were "chosen in Christ before the foundation of the world" (1.4). He is not stating that the church as a body was chosen in Christ but that individuals who by faith in Christ are members of that body were chosen "before the foundation of the world". God would have a people for His Son, who shall be holy and without blame before Him. To this end He chose them in accordance with His foreknowledge of them (see Rom. 8.29-30 and 1 Pet. 1.2). The believer rests secure on this great truth. He was chosen by God for salvation before the world was framed, called by God with an effective call in time, having been predestinated to sonship and heirship, to be conformed to the image of His Son. The eternal purpose of God was never placed at the mercy of man. He who works all things after the counsel of His own will does so to ensure that His purpose will never fail.

It is a great pity that these assuring truths, relating to such glorious matters, have become a theological battleground. As is so often the case, men have added logical extensions to, and raised philosophical objections against, revealed truth. The truth of election does not necessitate the addition of the erroneous doctrines of double predestination, limited atonement and the absence of a free offer in the gospel. Nor does it substantiate allegations of arbitrariness and capriciousness against God in the matter of salvation. Divine truth is often stated in extremes. To grasp the truth we must not seek to weave a middle path between the extremes but to grasp both ends of that spectrum of truth presented to us in the Scripture.

The objection is often raised as to how it could be equitable or right for God to choose some to be saved and at the same time hold responsible those who do not believe. Such an objection is invalid and futile as the Bible clearly teaches that God is sovereign and man is responsible. It is not for man to bring divine revelation to the bar of human reason and say that if it is not understood it cannot be right! That is a kind of intellectual arrogance that exposes its own paucity of faith and wisdom. Faith will always acknowledge that God is right at all times - even when His purposes and ways seem paradoxical. Faith will bow to revelation. And faith will bow to God who inhabits eternity.

This is the major point to grasp in connection with these truths. We see things only from the perspective of time but God, who is infinitely wise and omniscient, views things from the standpoint of eternity. As such He knows all things as present. Indeed, all things are present to Him in eternity because there is no succession in eternity. For this reason it is foolish to question the counsels, purposes, actions and ways of the eternal God. Man cannot fully enter into these things for such knowledge belongs to God alone: but man, by faith, can and must bow and worship before the One whose ways are perfect and say with the apostle, "O the depth of the riches both of the wisdom and knowledge of God! how unsearchable are His judgments, and His ways past finding out! For who hath known the mind of the Lord? or who hath been His counsellor? Or who hath first given to Him, and it shall be recompensed to him again? For of Him, and through Him, and to Him, are all things: to whom be glory for ever. Amen" (Rom. 11.33-36).

Every Bible doctrine has its use. It is relevant; it is not isolated from the life of the believer here on earth but is given for profit and right practice. As we apply the biblical teaching of the eternity of God we will each be able to live more for His glory.

Every believer will know times of feeling that there is nobody who understands him in his weakness. Isaiah ministered in the sure knowledge that there is One who knows and cares. He "fainteth not, neither is weary". "There is no searching of His understanding. He giveth power to the faint; and to them that have no might He increaseth strength". Who is this? He is the "everlasting God, the Lord, the Creator of the ends of the earth" (Is. 40.28-31). He cannot be likened to any other and though He is so great He has as the object of His care those who in their felt weakness wait upon Him. The One who faints not renews their strength so that they too shall not faint. And being eternal His power is not less than His will to be true to His word.

Because of the doctrine of God's eternity let us beware of having a love for the world that is passing. The Christian is now in enemy territory. We are not to love the world or the things that are in it. Both the world and the lust thereof pass away but the child of God has the capacity to do the will of God and in so doing abides for ever (1 Jn. 2.15-17). This world is not a fit place for the soul made, by grace, to have an interest in the eternity of God.

It was a common theme of Puritan writers that the eternal God is worthy of our choicest affections and of our best service. He has made us for His glory: our chief end is to glorify Him and to enjoy Him for ever. He is not found in the realm of human aggrandisement and self-seeking, or in the sphere where man vaunts himself as if he were God. God dwells with the humble and contrite and reveals Himself to faith. We must practise the presence of God; having done with lesser things, we must live out a life for His eternal glory.

Moses, the man of God, calls this to our attention. In contrast to the frailty of man Moses sees the eternal God. He looks at the mountains which appear solid and immovable. He notes the earth and the habitable world as being so mighty and yet recognises that One is greater than them all. He pre-dates creation and Moses therefore exclaims "from everlasting to everlasting Thou art God" (Ps. 90.2). Because of this Moses had a right estimation of himself. Frail, mortal man is as a sleep; he is like grass which grows. It flourishes; it is cut down; it withers. His days are spent as a tale that is told. So we must know our own weakness; we must know, too, the eternal foundations of our eternal God, so that His beauty may rest upon us.

This recurring theme of the Psalms is a granite foundation to secure our faith. We live in an uncertain world, where our immediate future is unknown and where the shifting sands of change and the lowering of standards might disturb us. One day the mountains and the earth will not be there any more. But God will. He is the refuge of His people in time of trouble; it is His name which is a strong tower, into which the righteous run and are safe (Prov. 18.10). That name is from everlasting (Is. 63.16); the refuge of His people is none other than "the eternal God" (Deut. 33.27). Beneath His troubled and afflicted people, surrounded as they are by their enemies, He places "His everlasting arms". Frail sense may well tremble at the oppression of the foe but faith will rest secure in the strength of the Eternal.

FURTHER READING

Classic Sermons on the Attributes of God. Compiled by W.W. Wiersbe. Kregel Publications. ISBN 0-8245-4038-6. Printed 1994

Discourses Upon the Existence and Attributes of God. S. Charnock. Baker Book House. Grand Rapids, Michigan. ISBN 0-8010-2437-4. 11th Printing, May 1993

Studies in Bible Doctrines. W. Hoste. John Ritchie Ltd. Printed 1948

The Attributes of God. A.W. Pink. Baker Book House. Grand Rapids, Michigan. ISBN 0-8010-6989-0. 31st Printing March 2000

The Glories of Our Lord. H.C. Hewlett. John Ritchie Ltd. ISBN 0-946351-41-4. Printed 1994

The Great Doctrines of the Bible. W. Evans. Moody Press. ISBN 0-8024-3096-1. Printed 1939

The Omniscience of Christ. R.E. Harlow, S. Hulshizer, R Oehm, A.M. Ure. Everyday Publications Inc. Ontario, Canada